INSIGHT GUIDES

MARRAKESH

Step by Step

APA PUBLICATIONS L
Part of the Langenscheidt Publishing Group

CONTENTS

ABOUT THIS BOOK

Above: Marrakesh, the 'Red City'.

This *Step by Step Guide* has been produced by the editors of Insight Guides, whose books have set the standard for visual travel guides since 1970. With top-quality photography and authoritative recommendations, it brings you the very best of Marrakesh in a series of 14 tailor-made tours.

WALKS AND TOURS

The tours provide something to suit all budgets, tastes and time frames. As well as covering Marrakesh's classic attractions, they track lesser-known sights, and there are also excursions outside the city to coastal Essaouira and the High Atlas region.

The tours embrace a range of interests, so whether you are an ardent shopper, an architecture buff, a gourmet or a garden lover, whether you have kids to entertain or are in need of pampering, you will find an option to suit.

We recommend that you read the whole of a tour before setting out. This should help you to familiarise yourself with the route and plan where to stop for refreshments – options for this are shown in the 'Food and Drink' boxes on most pages.

For our pick of the tours by theme, consult Recommended Tours For... *(see pp.6–7)*.

OVERVIEW

The tours are set in context by this introductory section, giving an overview of the city, plus background information on food and drink, shopping and other activities. A history timeline highlights the events that have shaped Marrakesh.

DIRECTORY

Supporting the tours is a Directory, with an A–Z of practical information, our pick of where to stay, and select restaurant listings to add to the cafés and restaurants that feature within the tours. Nightlife listings are also included here.

The Authors

Dorothy Stannard first got to know Marrakesh in the 1980s as a backpacker. She was bowled over by the city's exotic atmosphere and dramatic setting, and soon found herself coming back, at first purely for pleasure and later as a writer for guidebooks and the press. Over the years, Dorothy has seen the city change from a hippie haunt to a chic destination for wealthy second home-owners and a popular provider of short package breaks.

To cover the tours through the Atlas Mountains (tours 11–14), Dorothy enlisted the help of **Charlie Shepherd**, who first went to Marrakesh to build a hotel but ended up starting an adventure tour company specialising in hiking in the Atlas. Charlie also put his first-hand knowledge of Marrakesh's restaurant scene to good use by compiling the restaurant listings.

The book has been thoroughly revised for this 2nd edition by **Abigail Hole**, who first visited Marrakesh – now one of her favourite cities – almost 20 years ago, and has visited regularly ever since. A travel journalist, she has worked on numerous Africa guides, covering Morocco, Tunisia, Egypt, Mali and Mauritania.

Margin Tips
Shopping tips, handy hints, information on activities, key historical facts and interesting snippets help visitors to make the most of their time in Morocco.

Feature Boxes
Notable topics are highlighted in these special boxes.

Key Facts Box
This box gives details of the distance covered on the tour, plus an estimate of how long it should take. It also states where the tour starts and finishes, and gives key travel information such as which days are best to do the tour or handy transport tips.

Footers
Look here for the tour name, plus, where relevant, a map reference and also the main attraction on the double page.

Food and Drink
Recommendations of where to stop for refreshment are given in these boxes. The numbers prior to each restaurant/café name link to references in the main text. The restaurants are also plotted on the maps.

Restaurants are open daily, unless stated otherwise. The $ signs at the end of each entry reflect the approximate cost of a three-course meal for one, excluding drinks. These should be seen as a guide only. Price ranges, also quoted on the inside back flap for easy reference, are as follows:

$$$$ 500DH and above
$$$ 250–500DH
$$ 100–250DH
$ 100DH and below

Route Map
Detailed cartography shows the tour clearly plotted with numbered dots. For more detailed mapping, see the pull-out map slotted inside the back cover.

SHOPPERS

Spreading north of the Jemaa el Fna are Marrakesh's dazzling and extensive souks (walk 2). For chic boutiques explore the medina's Mouassine Quarter (walk 3) or wander down Rue de la Liberté in Guéliz (walk 6).

RECOMMENDED TOURS FOR...

ENTERTAINMENT

Jugglers, storytellers, acrobats, snake charmers, fortune tellers and trance musicians: the nightly entertainment on the Jemaa el Fna (walk 1) is one of the most exciting shows on earth.

CLASSIC CAFÉS

To get the measure of Marrakesh, watch the world go by from the Café de France on the Jemaa el Fna (walk 1) or the Café les Négociants in Guéliz (walk 6).

SPORTING ACTIVITIES

Ride or play golf in the Palmeraie (tour 7), hike up Mount Toubkal, the highest mountain in North Africa (tour 12), or try quad biking, kite-boarding and surfing in Essaouira (tour 10).

ARTS AND CRAFTS

As well as the splendid Museum of Marrakesh (walk 2), visit the Dar Si Said and eclectic Maison Tiskiwin (walk 4), and be sure to take in the excellent Islamic Arts Museum in the Majorelle Garden (walk 7).

ARCHITECTURE

Admire the 12th-century minaret of the Koutoubia Mosque (walk 1), be dazzled by the magnificent Ben Youssef Madrassa (walk 2), explore the labyrinthine El Bahia Palace (walk 4), and enjoy a mint tea in the authentically restored riad of Dar Cherifa (walk 3).

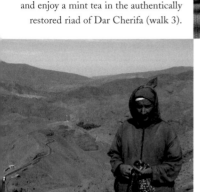

FABULOUS VIEWS

View the Jemaa el Fna from an upstairs terrace (walk 1), behold the Menara Pavilion framed against an Atlas backdrop (tour 8), watch the sun set from the walls of El Badi Palace (walk 5), and gaze at the dramatic scenery on a drive through the great Atlas passes (tours 12, 13 and 14).

PARKS AND GARDENS

An oasis on a desert plain, Marrakesh is renowned for its gardens, from the great Sultanic garden of the Menara (tour 8) to the magical Majorelle Garden (walk 7) to the grounds of La Mamounia Hotel, where Winston Churchill liked to paint (tour 8).

CHILDREN

As well as the evening entertainment on the Jemaa el Fna (walk 1), kids will enjoy a ride on a camel in the Palmeraie (tour 7), or a trip in a horse-drawn carriage (tour 9).

STRESS RELIEF

Loosen up in the sumptuous spas and hammams of Marrakesh (walk 5), lounge beside the pool at Nikki Beach in the Palmeraie (tour 7), or sink into the red leather seats of a calèche on a night-time *tour des remparts* (tour 9).

ORIENTATION

An overview of Marrakesh's geography, customs and culture, plus illuminating background information on food and drink, shopping, activities, pampering and history.

INTRODUCTION

Despite the city's recent modernisation and a commensurate increase in tourists, drawn by its fame, climate and exotic air, Marrakesh still offers a unique, multi-sensory North African experience.

The Medina
The old town of all Arab cities is known as the medina, after Medina in Arabia, the city where the Prophet Mohammed founded the first Islamic community. Unlike the New Town, Guéliz, with its straight, wide streets, Marrakesh's medina is a warren of tightly packed narrow alleyways and *derbs* (dead ends).

With all that Marrakesh has to offer, who wouldn't fall for the city? It has more than its fair share of the qualities that make a travel destination desirable, namely ease of access, year-round sunshine, a sublimely beautiful setting, an exotic – to Europeans – culture and lots of opportunities for pure self-indulgence.

DEVELOPMENT

Set on the Haouz Plain beneath the peaks of the High Atlas Mountains, the city spreads red and low in a sea of palms and olive groves. It was founded by the Almoravids, a Berber dynasty, in 1060, at the crossroads of intercontinental trade routes linking sea and desert. For merchants and travellers it was the first great city north of the Sahara.

The Red City

The adobe walls that the Almoravids built to enclose their settlement still form the basis for today's impressive ramparts. Extending for some 16km (10 miles) and entered by a dozen gates *(babs)*, they glow in the afternoon sun, earning Marrakesh the epithet the 'Red City'. Inside the walls is the medina (old town), centring on the Jemaa el Fna, a large irregular-shaped space ringed by cafés and filled with life,

intensity and magic; unlike other Moroccan cities, it has an exciting tang of sub-Saharan Africa.

West of the medina is the New Town, Guéliz, established by the French in 1912 following the creation of the French and Spanish protectorates. This is where most of the large hotels are located, particularly in the Hivernage area south of Avenue Mohammed V.

Marking the division between these two halves of the city is the Koutoubia Mosque, built by the Almohad Dynasty (1147–1248). The lovely minaret, with its distinctive brass pinnacle, is a useful orientation point day and night (when it is illuminated). From here it is a pleasant 30-minute walk along the broad and leafy Avenue Mohammed V to the heart of Guéliz, Place Abdel Moumen Ben Ali. Buses ply the route *(see p.55)*, and it is around 20DH by taxi.

Routes Out of the City

Beyond Guéliz routes head west and north, with a motorway stretching 600km (360 miles) to Tangier. South of Marrakesh roads lead to the two great passes through the High Atlas Mountains: the Tizi-n-Tichka to Ouarzazate and the Tizi-n-Test to Taroudant, gateways to Morocco's

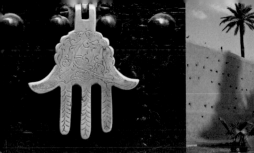

deep south and the Sahara. If these are closed after heavy snowfall, the only passage south is via the less interesting Imi-n-Tanoute to Agadir. There is no railway south of Marrakesh.

TOURISM BOOM

In recent years Marrakesh's profile as a tourist destination has soared. The city has long had its devotees, from Winston Churchill *(see p.62)* to Yves Saint Laurent to the Rolling Stones. But it was a programme of sustained investment and public initiatives (from parks and gardens to the construction of the Palais des Congrès conference venue and the Théâtre Royal); the liberalisation of property laws to encourage foreign buyers; the inauguration of an international film festival; and the introduction of budget airlines that turned the city from a well-kept secret of the aficionado to front-page news.

Fresh initiatives continue with the construction of a third airport terminal to open in 2012, and the spectacular renovation of La Mamounia, Morocco's most famous hotel. Riad property prices continue to rise, and tourist numbers were estimated at around 3.5 million in 2010.

PROPERTY

Hotel capacity in the city has increased massively over the last decade, with large chain hotels going up in the Hivernage area and the Palmeraie, and countless medina riads – traditional courtyard houses – being bought and restored by Western expats. The city has absorbed these additions surprisingly well. The large hotels are set well apart, in their own leafy enclave, and the riads are unobtrusive, their idyllic micro-worlds contained behind blank walls that are indistinguishable from surrounding buildings.

There is an ongoing debate about the pros and cons of gentrifying the medina, but by and large it is seen as preferable to the steady dereliction of the old town that had begun to set in as established *Marrakshi* families moved to more spacious properties in the New Town and the older properties were neglected.

Above from far left: Place des Epices; Berber woman; hand-shaped door-knocker to ward off the evil eye *(see p.42)*; city wall.

Below: entrance to a restored riad.

WORK, WORK, WORK

Marrakesh is the natural magnet for the High Atlas tribes who have migrated to the city in an attempt to make a better life. Small surprise then that the city has a reputation for hard work among other Moroccans; despite Marrakesh's holiday atmosphere, daily life here is considered tough, and traditionally people rise early and work late. Unlike Casablanca and Rabat, the city has few pretentions to sophistication and has a very small middle class.

ROYAL CONNECTIONS

In spite (or because) of this large working class, Marrakesh has long been a favourite getaway of the Moroccan royal family. The late King Hassan II (1929–99) spent a lot of time here (especially on the golf courses), and began the massive investment in the city that his son Mohammed VI consolidated. The Alaouite Dynasty, to which they belong, originated in the south of Morocco in the Tafilalt (a remote though well-populated valley south of the Atlas), and the family has tended to favour the 'capital of the south' over the more cultured cities of the north.

The extensive royal palace takes up a substantial chunk of the southern half of the medina (although Mohammed VI has built a new palace on Rue Sidi Mimoun), causing pedestrians to make long detours; as does the old Dar el Bacha (the former palace of Thami El Glaoui, aka the Pasha of Marrakesh, a tribal chief who colluded with the French in the first half of the 20th century) in the medina's northern half.

The Cult of King

Many buildings open to the public – offices, shops, restaurants, cafés – have a portrait of Mohammed VI on their walls. Although no longer all-but-obligatory as it was under the autocratic Hassan II, this practice reflects the huge reverence paid to the king as both head of state and 'Commander of the Faithful'. The latter title derives from the Alaouites' descent from the Prophet Mohammed and is the king's best weapon against Islamic radicalism.

RELIGION

For an Islamic country, Morocco is outwardly very tolerant, and Marrakesh particularly so. Despite much grinding poverty and the meagre benefits of

Right: the Kasbah Mosque's minaret.

trickle-down economics, it is hard to imagine hardline Islamicism taking root in easy-going Marrakesh. Alcohol is permitted, women dress as they please (although there are certainly many more covered heads than a decade ago), government censorship appears to be relatively light, and there is even an Ibiza-style nightclub (Pasha) on the city's southern outskirts.

But for the visitor to underestimate the importance of religion in the city would be a mistake. Mohammed VI's liberalisation of traditionally oriented family laws, derived from sharia, was fiercely resisted by large sections of society. The mosques, too, are busy, even in the city centre. As the muezzin's call to sunset prayer reverberates around the Jemaa el Fna, the musicians and entertainers fall silent, and a surprising number of people drift off into the mosques to pray.

A GARDEN CITY

Despite being situated on a dry and stony plain, with little rainfall even in winter, Marrakesh is an extraordinarily green city. Underground springs gave life to the Palmeraie, a date plantation off the Casablanca road, many centuries ago, and successive dynasties mastered the art of irrigation, tapping into the water table to create orchards, olive groves and palace gardens.

In his travelogue *Escape with Me!* (1939), the British writer Osbert Sitwell called Marrakesh the 'ideal African city of water-lawns, cool, pillared palaces and orange groves'. Today, visiting gardeners will find lots to interest them in the Majorelle Garden, El Bahia Palace, La Mamounia Hotel and the Cyber Parc, from towering cacti to poinsettia trees – striking full-grown versions of the ubiquitous Christmas pot plants.

Above from far left: shoppers in one of the city's souks; a herbalist on the Jemaa el Fna; the Cyber Parc in Guéliz; Majorelle Garden.

Private Views Morocco Telecom has banned the use of Google Earth in Morocco, fearing, it's believed, that users would be able to spy on Mohammed VI's extensive palaces.

A Feudal Land

Every year the king's sovereignty is underlined in the Act of Allegiance, a centuries-old ceremony in which tribal chiefs, religious leaders and high-ranking officials pledge their loyalty and obedience by bowing low and kissing the sovereign's hand. In many other monarchies, this might seem like a cherished tradition redolent of a bygone age, but in Morocco it is an accurate reflection of the country's feudal nature. In spite of Mohammed VI's modernising moves since acceding to the throne and his eschewal of the method of operation of his father (an oriental potentate with an extensive harem etc), he remains all-powerful. Although there are multi-party elections, the king personally appoints the prime minister, senior ministers and judges, is head of the armed forces, and, as 'Commander of the Faithful', is spiritual leader too.

FOOD AND DRINK

Thanks to the boom in tourism, it is now possible to enjoy a wide range of cuisines in Marrakesh. However, many visitors find that the wealth of Moroccan food on offer is enough to tantalise the palate for their entire stay.

Gone are the days when dining out in Marrakesh was a choice between French classics in a old-fashioned restaurant in Guéliz or a *couscous royale* in a cavernous and half-empty *palais* in the medina. Now you can also enjoy Italian, Spanish, Japanese, Indian, Thai and modern European food in stylish settings. Top chefs have been drawn to the city, such as Michelin-starred Fabrice Vulin, whose Dar Ennasim *(see p.120)*, overlooking the lake at the Pavillon du Golf in the Palmeraie, serves innovative French cuisine.

MOROCCAN CUISINE

International interest in Moroccan cuisine has taken it out of the home and into some very sophisticated restaurant kitchens, where it is often fused with other influences to create exciting new tastes. Flavoursome meat, fruit and vegetables, and top-quality fish rushed in at the crack of dawn from Essaouira and Agadir, also make Marrakesh an interesting place for cooks and gourmets. Indeed, several enterprising riad-owners specialise in providing Moroccan cookery lessons in addition to the usual programme of excursions and activities *(see margin, left)*.

Cookery Lessons
Several hotels and riads offer their guests (and non-residents) Moroccan cookery lessons. Among the best regarded are La Maison Arabe *(see p.111)*, near Bab Doukkala, and Jnane Tamsna in the Palmeraie *(see p.113)*.

STREET FOOD

At the other end of the scale, the Moroccan pleasure in food is reflected in the amazing array of snacks sold from makeshift stands on street corners or hawked by a vast army of vendors. Cauldrons of snails in a cumin-flavoured liquor (try the Jemaa el Fna or the Place des Epices), pans of freshly made tortilla, trays of soft sugared doughnuts *(sfenj)*, newspaper cones of freshly roasted nuts or handmade potato crisps (quite possibly fried in a sawn-off oil drum) are just a few of the tasty temptations encountered on a stroll through the medina.

Everything is beautifully displayed, from the pyramids of glistening olives and vibrantly coloured spices in the markets to skewers of succulent lamb fresh off the grill and fanned out on a palm leaf.

STAPLE DISHES

In restaurants, the once-ubiquitous couscous has lost out to the highly versatile tajine in the popularity stakes, but it remains a firm favourite in Moroccan homes, especially at lunchtime on Friday, when it is traditionally served after prayers at the Friday Mosque.

Couscous and Tajines

Couscous is usually topped with a stew of chicken or lamb, chickpeas, courgettes, turnips, tomatoes and carrots, and accompanied by a glass of *laban* (a sour-tasting cultured milk).

Tajines – tasty stews served in distinctive pots with conical lids – come in many delicious guises, and are where many of the subtleties and surprises of Moroccan cuisine are found. They frequently pair sweet and savoury, or savoury and sour, with knockout results. Typical combinations are beef with quinces, lamb with dates and apricots, or beef with almonds and whole hard-boiled eggs. One of the most common tajines is chicken with preserved lemons and olives *(djej maqalli)*.

The meat is always cooked slowly in large slabs or on the bone, and presented in a large flat dish placed in the centre of the table, to which everyone tucks in. Small dishes of olives, sliced and salted cucumber, roasted aubergine mashed with garlic, lemon and olive oil, mixed pickles and other salads are served on the side, along with warm flatbread.

Pastilla

More unusual, as it is time-consuming and difficult to make, is *pastilla*, a dish of layered *warkha* pastry interleaved with pounded pigeon breast, mixed with saffron, egg, spices and almonds, and finished with a dusting of icing sugar. Traditionally a festive dish, good *pastilla* can be ordered in the more exclusive restaurants; an average restaurant is unlikely to do it well.

Sweets

At home, meals normally end with fruit followed by mint tea *(see margin, p.16)* and a selection of home-made sweets. These tend to be made of filo pastry, with honey, dates, figs, almonds or pistachios, although nowadays chocolate is also popular. 'Gazelles' horns' (crescents of sweet pastry with an almond and semolina filling) are typical. Plain sweetened yoghurt, often home-made, or ricotta mixed with honey and sesame are other great ways to finish a meal. Shopbought European-style pastries, with confectioner's custard and fancy glazes, are often bought for special occasions.

Above from far left: tajines; lamb with potatoes and peas; Moroccan flatbread; dried fruit stall on the Jemaa el Fna.

Below: pastries.

Ramadan Specialities

Ramadan may be the month of fasting, but the daily breaking of the fast at sundown is eagerly anticipated and several special dishes are served during this time. The most important is *harira*, a meaty soup (lamb or chicken) with chickpeas and sometimes egg, flavoured with chopped coriander and a squeeze of lemon juice. Almost everyone ends their fast with a bowlful, sometimes accompanied by dates and milk, followed by *shebakkia (pictured)*, knots of deep-fried pastry dipped in honey or syrup and sprinkled with sesame seeds. If you want to try *harira* outside Ramadan, several of the food-stalls on the Jemaa el Fna serve it.

DRINKS

Global brands of soft and alcoholic drinks are available: Heineken is the most common imported beer, but you will find a fair selection of labels in the more fashionable clubs and bars. Locally made juices, beer and wine are definitely worth sampling, though.

Fresh Juices

The orange-juice sellers on the Jemaa el Fna are as much a part of the scene as the acrobats and snake charmers, and at some point in your stay you are bound to buy a glass from them. It is best (and cheapest) during winter, when you will pay about 12DH for a glass on the square and about double in

Time for Tea
Moroccans attach as much ceremony to the drinking of tea as the Japanese or British do. Brewed in distinctive silver-coloured teapots with fresh mint and sugar, it is poured into delicate glasses, often from a height to cool and aerate the steaming liquid. Mint tea (*thé à la menthe*) hits the spot at any time of day, but it is especially good as a digestive.

cafés and restaurants. Fresh apple, pear, banana, almond and even avocado juices (the last two sweetened and liquidised with milk) are all available in season. Sugar is often added automatically, so if you don't want it, be sure to say so, though you might find a small amount is nicer than none.

Beers and Wines

Alcohol is served in the more expensive restaurants and café-bars, hotels and nightclubs. Until fairly recently, it was impossible to buy alcohol in the medina, but laws were relaxed when the riad phenomenon took hold, and you will now find late-night drinking haunts such as Kosybar *(see p.48)*, overlooking Place des Ferblantiers in the heart of the old town. The national brews are Flag, Stork and Casablanca, lager-type bottled beers that sell for 40–60DH depending on the venue.

Moroccan wine has come a long way in recent years. It is mainly produced around Meknes and Casablanca. Good reds include Coteaux de l'Atlas, Beni M'Tir Larroque Cabernet Sauvignon and Merlot blend, and Médaillon Cabernet from the Domaine des Ouled Thaleb vineyard. Whites to try include Beauvallon Chardonnay from the Beni M'Tir vineyard and the Médaillon Cabernet Blanc. A recommended place to sample Moroccan wines is Kosybar *(see above)*. The owner's father is the proprietor of the award-winning Les Celliers de Meknes vineyard, and he has a good selection of both their own and other wines.

The Moroccan Menu

Above from far left: orange-juice carts; a selection of tasty brochettes.

bessara	Broad (fava) beans mashed with paprika, cumin, oil, garlic and olive oil.
briouats	Delicious deep-fried envelopes of *warkha* (filo) pastry filled with minced lamb and herbs, cheese or egg.
brochettes	Lamb, chicken, beef or liver grilled on skewers over charcoal. Brochette stands are everywhere, and on major roads, grill restaurants, serving brochettes, *merguez*, *kefta* and lamb cutlets, cluster around junctions.
couscous	Morocco's national dish: a meat, vegetable and chickpea stew on a steaming bed of semolina grains. Fish and vegetable couscous also found. Two popular kinds of couscous include one with seven vegetables and another with caramelised onions, raisins and chickpeas.
douara	Tasty casserole of marinated lamb's tripe, liver and heart, popular after Aid el Kebir festival when each family buys and slaughters a lamb.
harira	Moroccan soup of lamb, lentils, chickpeas, noodles, egg and more, spiced with cinnamon, ginger, cayenne, turmeric and coriander.
harissa	A spicy red-pepper sauce often served with grilled meats.
hergma	Calves' feet. A few stalls on the Jemaa el Fna specialise in this delicacy.
hout/samek	The Arabic words for fish (*tagine bel hout*, for example, is a fish tajine), but on menus fish is usually listed by type in French: *thon* (tuna), *loup de mer* (sea bass), *rouget* (red mullet), *dorade* (sea bream), *merlan* (whiting), *homard* (lobster), and *crevettes* (prawns). A spicy *chermoula* marinade is sometimes used to improve the taste of large white fish.
kefta	Meatballs flavoured with coriander and cumin, and often served with a fried egg and *harissa* on the side. A widely available great-tasting standby.
khobz	Bread. Mainly comes in two kinds: French or small, flat wholemeal loaves.
laban	A sour-tasting cultured milk that is traditionally served with couscous.
mechoui	A dish of spit-roasted lamb for special occasions. Often served at oriental entertainments such as Chez Ali *(see p.23)*.
merguez	Spicy lamb or beef sausages, sometimes served with fried eggs or as part of a mixed grill, with a dollop of *harissa*.
pastilla	An intricate pigeon pie made with layered *warkha* pastry and topped with a dusting of sugar. There is also chicken *pastilla* and fish *pastilla*.
samek	See *hout*.
tajine	The name for both the cooking vessel and the recipe, the latter being a tasty stew of meat and vegetables. Variations include chicken with lemon and olives, beef with prunes and almonds, lamb with dates and apricots.

SHOPPING

The extensive souks of Marrakesh are very much a highlight of a visit to Morocco. But the city also has a sprinkling of chic boutiques and an out-of-town shopping quarter showcasing the best of modern Moroccan design.

Trading Hours
Shops in the souks follow no set hours, but most open Sat–Thur 10am–8pm (some, but by no means all, close for a long lunch from around 1pm) and Fri 10am–noon. Shops in Guéliz open 10am–1.30pm and 3.30–7.30pm and close on Sunday.

Marrakesh has lived by trade for centuries. Built on the crossroads of global caravan routes, and the chief trading centre for the tribes of the High Atlas, it has long been a place where raw materials have been bought and sold and then turned into luxury goods that can also be traded.

The best times to shop are the morning, when business is brisk and efficient, and early evening when *Marrakshis* pour into the souks not just to buy but to browse and soak up the atmosphere: the gorgeous colours, the twinkling lights, the smell of mint and spices.

Traditionally in Morocco, the men in the family do the shopping, perhaps to shield their wives from the cut and thrust of the marketplace, perhaps to control the purse strings. While this is no longer so true, you will still see more men than women in the souks.

Below: the smell of fresh mint is one of the many aromas you will encounter in the souks.

WHERE TO SHOP

The Main Souks
Like other ancient Islamic cities, Marrakesh has an extensive network of souks where goods are made and sold side by side. Stretching north of the Jemaa el Fna, they cover an area of about 4 sq km (1½ sq miles), a vast labyrinth, partially roofed by makeshift mats or boards, which can quickly disorientate first-time visitors. Walk 2 *(see pp.34–9)* picks out the main areas and arteries of this part of the old city.

For visitors, the most relevant and interesting sections of the souk remain the Souk des Babouches (slippers); Souk Cherratine (leather); Kissarias (a series of small shopping arcades, mainly selling textiles); Souk Haddadine (which means 'blacksmiths' but nowadays sells a mixture of goods, from ceramics to clothes); and Souk des Teinturiers (dyers).

One of the most attractive corners of the souk, and itself worth a morning's exploration, is Place des Epices, domain of the herbalists but also filled with women selling baskets, bags and hats (straw in summer and colourful rough woollen caps in winter).

Other Interesting Souks
For lanterns in all shapes and sizes, as well as other brasswork being made and sold, visit the attractive Place des Ferblantiers at the foot of Rue Riad Zitoun el Jdid *(see p.48)* on the southern side of the medina. Also close by is the Grande Bijouterie, a slender alleyway of tiny shops crammed with amazingly ornate gold jewellery *(see p.48)*.

The Mouassine Quarter

Reflecting its more refined character, the area west of the Mouassine Mosque has a number of small individual boutiques selling more unusual items – such as clothes, gifts and tableware – often based on traditional crafts but given a contemporary twist. Rue el Ksour *(see p.40)* is worth a wander in this regard. Also in the Mouassine area is the Ministero del Gusto (near Villa Flore, Derb Azzouz), an interior design shop-cum-gallery set up by the designer Fabrizio Bizzari and Alessandro Lippini, a former style editor on Italian *Vogue*.

Guéliz

Some of the side streets off Avenue Mohammed V are worth exploring, in particular Rue de la Liberté *(see pp.56–7)*, which crosses the avenue just south of Place Abdel Moumen Ben Ali. It has several interior decor shops, an up-market spa, fine-quality pastry shops, a good leather store and several jewellers that offer more refined versions of traditional pieces than the Grande Bijouterie. Also off Mohammed V, near Place du 16 Novembre, is Plaza Marrakech, a new shopping precinct that is slowly filling with international fashion and sportswear shops. Similarly good for luxury goods and designer wear is the Centre Commercial Kawkab, a smart mall in the Hivernage area.

Sidi Ghanem Industrial Zone

If you are seriously interested in contemporary Moroccan design, or are looking to export larger traditional pieces such as well-made *zellige* (mosaic-tiled) table-tops, wrought-iron garden furniture or tiles, pay a visit to the purpose-built Sidi Ghanem Industrial Zone, off Route de Safi (northwest exit from the city). Ask at your hotel or riad for a map that includes a plan of the district, and negotiate with a taxi for a half-day trip here; this should cost around 300–400DH return, including waiting time.

Above from far left: daylight filters into a busy souk; a lamp emporium.

The Art of Haggling

Haggling is an intrinsic part of Moroccan culture, which visitors to Morocco either embrace and enjoy, or loathe to such a degree that they avoid shopping altogether. There are no hard-and-fast rules to this mindgame, other than never start haggling for something you have no intention of buying (time-wasters are not tolerated kindly) and start your negotiations at well below the asking price (a third, or even a quarter, is often suggested).

If you don't enjoy haggling, you could seek out the fixed-price government-run shop Ensemble Artisanal, opposite the Cyber Parc on Avenue Mohammed V *(see p.55)*. Most shops in Guéliz also display price tags, but even here, don't be afraid to make the shopkeeper an offer (although not substantially below the asking price). The only thing one doesn't haggle for, even in markets, is food.

Among the showrooms are Akkal (no. 322) for stunning ceramics and textiles; Via Notti (next door to Akkal) and Angie (no. 391), both of which sell fine linens and other fabrics; Amira Bougies (no. 277), offering handmade statement candles; and Atelier Nihal (no. 366), which sells stylish cushions, throws and other soft furnishings.

For some new slants on traditional Moroccan carpets, visit Talamanzou (932 Résidence al Massar, Route de Safi, located on the right-hand side of the Safi road as you leave town; tel: 0524-33 53 35).

Picking a Carpet
Carpets sold in markets are both machine- and hand-made; it is better to visit one of the more reputable carpet shops, such as Bazaar du Sud in Souk des Tapis, off Place des Epices, if you want one of the latter. Examine the back of the carpet: a genuine handwoven rug will be far from perfectly finished.

WHAT TO BUY

Carpets and Blankets

Carpets are sold in all quarters of the souks, but especially in Souk des Tapis, off Place des Epices. Chichaoua and Sidi Moktar, on the way to Essaouira, are also considered good places to buy carpets.

You will find tufted carpets and *kilims* (flat-weave rugs), often in shades of red and yellow, with geometric patterns and symbols such as lozenges, crosses and stylised eyes to deflect *djinn* (supernatural spirits).

Ceramics

Several of the more up-market shops in Guéliz (L'Orientaliste, 11 and 15 Rue de la Liberté; La Porte d'Orient, 6 Boulevard el Mansour Eddahbi) have stunning (and expensive) traditional and/or antique tableware for sale (usually from Fez and Meknes). But for cheaper versions, examine the items displayed along the exit roads from town. Like carpets, the massive serving plates and vases can be hard to resist, but note that they tend to chip quite easily. The glazed tajine pots are for serving tajines rather than cooking them, though the earthenware ones can be used over charcoal and often come with a stand to hold the hot coals. Beware patio pots that will not withstand frost.

You may also find inexpensive earthenware cups decorated with a black resin derived from the thuya tree *(see Woodwork, right)*. The resin's distinctive medicinal smell has the advantage of repelling insects.

Edibles

Argan oil is widely sold, both in Marrakesh and in Essaouira, where it is produced from the fruit of argan

trees, a thorny low-growing tree that is found only in this region *(see p.95)*. The oil is used in cooking but is also valued for its skin-healing properties and is used in soaps, face creams and other beauty products.

A selection of Moroccan sweets makes a good gift to take home. There are plenty of shops where you can buy them, but check out the ones in Rue de la Liberté in Guéliz or visit Amandine *(see p.56)*.

Other edibles worth buying are olives, of which there are many varieties and almost as many different ways of preparing them, and jars of preserved lemons (a staple of Moroccan cuisine). Investigate the Marché Central, off Avenue Mohammed V (behind Plaza Marrakech) in Guéliz.

Leatherware

Moroccan leather is of very good quality. For the most dazzling displays of *babouches*, the soft slippers with the turned-down heel, visit the Souk des Babouches *(see p.36)* in the northern half of the medina. The slippers range from the very glamorous – sequin-encrusted, embroidered with silver thread, and in many gorgeous colours – to the utilitarian brown, red or yellow varieties for men. White *babouches* are traditionally worn to the Friday Mosque. Jackets, handbags, briefcases, lampshades and pouffes are found everywhere. In Guéliz, Place Vendôme (141 Avenue Mohammed V, at the corner of Rue de la Liberté) has a good selection of quality items.

Metalware

This is a speciality of Marrakesh. Items range from massive brass door-knockers and hinges to wrought-iron furniture and grilles, and from the curvy silver-coloured teapots (ideal souvenirs) to highly patterned copper or brass trays and vases that cover every inch of many an Aladdin's cave. The quality varies tremendously, but it is not difficult to get a sense of this. For decorative lanterns seek out Place des Ferblantiers *(see p.48)*.

For quality decorative items try the better bazaars in the souks, or shops such as L'Orientaliste and La Porte d'Orient *(see Ceramics, left)*, which also sell some amazing examples of antique Berber jewellery: massive brooches and *kuhl-kahl* (anklets), necklaces, earrings and rings.

Woodwork

Sections of old doors, *mashrabiyyah* screens, and old painted wooden chests and tables have become much sought-after in recent years. Shops such as La Porte d'Orient *(see Ceramics, left)* have some very fine examples. However, you will also find such items in the souks, though be aware that 'antique' pieces may simply be expertly distressed.

Much cheaper are the many different items (from hair slides to chess sets and furniture) made from the distinctively marked thuya wood of the Essaouira region; however, be aware that the indigenous tree from which this comes is endangered. It's best to buy any such products from environmentally conscious cooperatives.

Above from far left: slippers in the Souk des Babouches; glazed ceramic plates; mounds of spices.

Feel-Good Shopping
Support others as you shop by visiting Marrakesh's fixed-price cooperatives. Al Kawtar is an embroidery work-shop for disabled women that offers apprenticeships in stitching and provides day care and meals. You can visit their embroidery workshop (3 Derb Zaoua Laftiha) in the Medina, or the boutique (57 rue Laksour), which sells exquisitely embroidered table linens, towels and clothes.

Below: jars of preserved fruits and vegetables; olives aplenty.

ACTIVITIES

Marrakesh has found all kinds of ways to entertain its visitors, from climbing the highest mountain in North Africa to taking an exciting new look at the city by hot-air balloon.

Ballooning
You will need a clear winter's day for full effect, but a bird's-eye view of the 'Red City', the surrounding palm groves and the snow-clad Atlas could prove the most memorable part of your stay in Marrakesh. The flights offered by Ciel d'Afrique (15 Rue de Mauritanie, Guéliz; tel: 0524-43 28 43; www.cieldafrique.info) cost slightly more than 2,000DH per person (half-price for children under 10), plus extra for breakfast, champagne etc. Morocco Adventure Tours (tel: 0659-34 67 03; www.morocco adventuretours.com) offers ballooning trips over the Ourika Valley for £180.

Marrakesh is the ideal sybarite's city – it doesn't have too many 'sights', it offers year-round fine weather that is perfect for poolside lounging, and it has plenty of restaurants and spas for fine dining and pampering. But should you find yourself raring to do something active, you will not be disappointed either.

CULTURAL EVENTS

The city has few cultural facilities in the European sense, but there is more going on than is at first apparent, and the best way to find out about events is to look in the free monthly *Couleurs Marrakech* (www.couleurs-marrakech. com), available in hotels and restaurants.

The most active venues are the Théâtre Royal, at 40 Boulevard Mohammed VI in Guéliz, which stages concerts and dance as well as exhibitions, and the Institut Français *(see p.56)* on the Route de Targa (extension of Avenue Mohammed V), which organises concerts, films, exhibitions and plays (albeit in French).

Other events – exhibitions, concerts, jazz evenings – are held in Dar Cherifa *(see p.41)* and also in café-restaurants such as the Café du Livre *(see p.56)*, Le Grand Café de la Poste (beside the main post office, off Place du 16 Novembre; *see p.119*) and various hotels.

In December each year, Marrakesh holds an International Film Festival, (www.festivalmarrakech.info), with films shown in various venues, including the Palais des Congrès on Avenue Mohammed VI, and on the Jemaa el Fna, where a specially erected giant screen can be viewed by all for free.

HIKING AND BIKING

Marrakesh is the natural springboard for treks in the Atlas, and in particular the Toubkal National Park *(see p.79)*. If you have not come on a trekking holiday but would like to sample the Atlas terrain, it is easy to arrange something once you have arrived in the country, whether you just want a one-day hike in the foothills, a three-day hike to Toubkal's summit, or something altogether longer.

You can arrange an exhilarating trip hiking, canyoning, white-water rafting or quad biking through Morocco Adventure Tours (tel: 0659-34 67 03; www.moroccoadventuretours.com), or hiking through Mountain Voyage Morocco (5 Avenue Mohammed V, Guéliz; tel: 0524-42 19 96; www. mountain-voyage.com). Alternatively, head up to Imlil and make arrangements independently on the spot. The cost of hiring a mountain guide, who can organise food, mules and equipment if

necessary, and staying in mountain lodges *(gites)* is set and published by the tourist board. The best time for hiking is late spring through to early autumn.

GOLF

Morocco has some very good courses, including three in Marrakesh – each of them beautifully situated. Expect to pay about 500DH for 18 holes, plus 300DH green fees.

The Royal Golf Club (Route de Ouarzazate; tel: 0524-40 47 05) is set just 5km (3 miles) south of the city. Dating from 1918, Marrakesh's original 18-hole golf course has welcomed Churchill and Eisenhower and was a favourite of the late King Hassan II.

Backed by the Atlas Mountains, Amelkis (Route de Ouarzazate; tel: 0524-40 44 14) is an 18-hole course 7km (4 miles) south of the city.

Slightly further out of town (8km/ 5 miles) is the Palmeraie Golf Club (Palmeraie; tel: 0524-36 87 66; www. pgpmarrakech.com). Like many of Morocco's top golf courses, this was designed by Robert Trent Jones.

HORSE RIDING

Marrakesh's Palmeraie, Essaouira's beach and the foothills of the Atlas Mountains all offer wonderful terrain for horse riding. There are also specialist tour companies offering one- and two-week riding holidays, and several hotels in the Atlas can arrange riding for their guests. Expect to pay around 200DH per hour or 500DH for half a day.

The Atlas à Cheval ranch (932 Residence Al Massar, Route de Safi; tel: 0524-36 86 10; http://atlasacheval-marrakech.net) is situated among olive groves about 26km (16 miles) from Marrakesh. It offers good half- and full-day treks into the surrounding hills.

In Essaouira, the Ranch d'Essaouira (Diabet; tel: 0676-92 52 11; www. ranchdessaouira.com) provides a wide range of treks, including a half-day (5-hour) trek along the coast plus two-, three- and six-day treks, with overnight accommodation in communal tents. They also offer camel rides and quad-bike trips.

SURFING, WINDSURFING, KITE-BOARDING

Essaouira has been a popular destination for surfers for decades. The best conditions for surfing are at Moulay Bouzerktoun, 20km (12 miles) to the north, and Sidi Kaouki, 27km (17 miles) to the south.

The Ocean Vagabond café (not the guesthouse) on Essaouira's beach is a good place to find out about water sports in the area; it also hires out windsurfing equipment and body boards. Ocean Vagabond Base Nautique (located on the beach; tel: 0524-78 39 34; www.ocean vagabond.com) offers surfing, windsurfing and kite-boarding lessons; Magic Fun Afrika (22-2 Rue Ibn Azim; tel: 0524-47 38 56; www.magicfunafrika. com) offers lessons and equipment hire for kite-boarding, surfing, windsurfing and kayaking. Tuition and equipment hire cost from 200DH per hour.

Above from far left: musicians in Le Comptoir, a restaurant and club; the Royal Golf Club; ascending Mount Toubkal.

For Families
Most children will find plenty of amusement on the Jemaa el Fna, or taking camel rides in the Palmeraie.

There is also the Oasiria waterpark (Route du Barrage, 4km; tel: 0524-38 04 38; www.oasiria.com; Apr–early Sept 10am–6pm; charge, small children free), situated on the road to Asni, 4km (2½ miles) from town, which offers giant slides, wave machines, a fake beach and a pirate pool for smaller children.

A treat for the whole family, Chez Ali (Palmeraie; tel: 0524-30 77 30; www.chez alimarrakech.com) offers a three-hour oriental extravaganza held every evening in the Palmeraie on the outskirts of town. Dine on *mechoui* (a ceremonial dish of roast lamb) and be entertained by dancers, musicians, acrobats and a fantasia (a traditional entertainment of charging horsemen).

PAMPERING

Having long enjoyed the traditional Moroccan hammam, the 'Marrakshis' have been quick to meet the constant demand for pampering among stressed-out foreign visitors.

Mixed Bathing
Contrary to the modest customs of traditional hammams, the luxurious Bains de Marrakech *(see p.52)* allows couples to visit the hammam together, providing they book a private room.

THE HAMMAM EXPERIENCE

Until fairly recently, only the wealthiest Moroccan homes had a properly equipped bathroom. Although people kept clean by washing with a jug and a bowl of water – ritual ablutions alone demand that Muslims wash five times a day before prayers – most of them went once a week to their local hammam for a thorough steam and *gommage* (exfoliation). Bathrooms are now far more widespread, but most Moroccans continue to go to their local hammam, partly for the deep-pore cleansing that domestic showers can't quite provide, but also for the social aspect of a visit.

For women, in particular, going to the hammam has always been a jolly social occasion, where, with children in tow, they can meet with their friends, gossip and joke, and might even take a sneaky look to check out which potential brides might be suitable for male members of their family.

For Moroccan men, the hammam tends to be a more sombre place of rest and contemplation, where the week's mental stress is relieved and the resident masseur sets to work on relieving the knotty tensions in their back and shoulders.

Tourist Luxury

In recent years, for foreigners at least, the humble Moroccan hammam has evolved into a place of luxury and even decadence – a sumptuous spa with deep blue pools, petal-strewn divans and state-of-the-art treatments that can rejuvenate even the most work-worn customer. As a rule, these are intended for tourists who want to indulge in an oriental fantasy and try out the fabulous-sounding treatments (a 'Thousand and One Nights pedicure', a 'Mint-tea Wrap') that would be far more expensive at home.

Local Hammams

Neighbourhood hammams, usually attached to the local bakery in order to share its furnace, are of varying quality. Some of the more venerable hammams, particularly those attached to the more ancient mosques, are handsome buildings with carved cedar ceilings, star-shaped skylights and other decorative features; others are Stygian places that seem more like breeding areas for germs than places of purification. In between is a host of functional modern establishments.

If you try a local hammam, you will find there is a changing area leading into a series of rooms of varying temperature, and you will be given a

bucket for sluicing down. If you forget to take your own bar, locals are often happy to share soap (the traditional black kind) and other equipment; the masseur (a massage is included in the price) will find you at some point during your stay to give you a good *gommage* and pummelling.

A RANGE OF HAMMAMS

A selection of hammams in the Kasbah area (including one or two small establishments attached to riads) is given in Tour 5 *(see p.52)*. These include the luxurious Bains de Marrakech *(see margin, left)*.

Hotel Spas

Among the big hotels, Es Saadi (Avenue el Qadissia, Hivernage area; tel: 0524-44 88 11; www.essaadi.com) and L'Hivernage Hotel and Spa (corner of Avenue Echouhada and Rue des Temples; tel: 0524-42 41 00; www.hivernage-hotel.com) are particularly noted for their spas, although most of the large hotels and the more exclusive riads have spa facilities.

Popular Choices

Less luxurious but well-run, clean and functional is Hammam Ziani (14 Rue Riad Zitoun el Jdid; tel: 0524-37 53 78; www.hammamziani.ma), near El Bahia Palace. In Guéliz one of the best-run spas, popular with well-heeled *Marrakshis*, is Les Secrets de Marrakech, (62 Rue de la Liberté; tel: 0524-43 48 48), offering all sorts of tempting facials, massages and wraps. If you would like to try a good local hammam, check out the 16th-century hammam next to the Doukkala Mosque. Like many smaller hammams, it is open to men in the morning and evening, and women in the afternoon.

One for Women

Lastly, women may want to try out the Le Cinq Sens (72 Place Jemaa el Fna, next to the Café de France; tel: 0678-82 80 40). It is not a hammam or spa, but a spotless, well-run beauty salon where you can get a top-to-toe makeover (half-hour massage with argan oil, facial, manicure and blow-dry) for an all-in very low price of around 500DH, and good-quality henna tattoos from 60DH.

Above from far left: candlelit bathroom at Riad Magi; La Sultana is a riad with a spa attached *(see p.52)*; floating candles and flowers; La Sultana.

Hammam Etiquette
Up-market hammams provide everything you will need, and are fairly relaxed about nudity. Local hammams require you to take your own soap, scrubbing mitt and towel, and you're expected to keep your briefs on. It is usual to tip the various attendants a few dirhams.

HISTORY: KEY DATES

*Marrakesh's fortunes have depended upon the tastes of the ruling dynasties.
It was beautified by the Almoravids, Almohads and Saadians, ignored by the
Merenids, but found favour again under Hassan II and Mohammed VI.*

PRE-ISLAM

Below: the Almohads were able to capture Marrakesh through Bab Ghemat in 1147; El Badi Palace was built by Saadian sultan Ahmed el Mansour in the 16th century; members of the Saadian dynasty were laid to rest in a complex of elegant tombs.

1100s BC	Phoenician sailors establish a series of trading posts along Morocco's coast, including Karikon Telichos (modern-day Essaouira).
146BC	Carthage falls to Rome. Roman influence spreads west through North Africa.
AD682	First Arab raids on Morocco under the command of Oqba ibn Nafi.

ISLAM AND THE DYNASTIES

714	Further Arab incursions into Morocco and Spain. Berbers embrace Islam and invade Spain under Arab leadership.
788	Idriss I, exiled from Baghdad, founds Morocco's first Arab dynasty.
807	Idriss II founds Fez.
1060–1147	The Almoravids, Berber warriors from modern-day Mauritania, sweep north, founding Marrakesh as their capital.
1147	The Almohad dynasty, also Berber, rise out of the High Atlas and seize power. They build the Giralda in Seville, the Koutoubia in Marrakesh and the Tour Hassan in Rabat.
1230	The Almohad Sultan el Mamoun accepts 12,000 Christian cavalry from King Ferdinand of Castile and Leon to retake Marrakesh from dissidents. A Catholic church is built in the city for foreign mercenaries.
1248	The Merenids, also Berber, rise up from the Sahara and conquer Fez, which they make their capital. Muslim and Jewish refugees arrive, fleeing the Inquisition in Spain.
1269	The Merenids conquer Marrakesh. They build a *madrassa* next to the Ben Youssef Mosque (later replaced by the Saadian *madrassa*).
1492	Fall of Muslim Spain.
1554–1669	The Arab Saadian dynasty drives out the Christians. They base themselves in Marrakesh, building the Saadian Tombs, El Badi Palace and the Ben Youssef Madrassa, and establish the *mellah*.
1669	Beginning of the present Alaouite dynasty.
1672–1727	Brutal but effective rule under Moulay Ismail in Meknes.
1866	El Bahia Palace is built.

EUROPEAN ENCROACHMENT

1894–1908 Sultan Abdelaziz leaves Morocco bankrupt and wide open to European encroachment.

1912 The Treaty of Fez. Morocco is carved up between France and Spain. In Marrakesh General Lyautey, the first Resident General, establishes the French-built New Town, known as Guéliz.

1920s Thami el Glaoui, Pasha of Marrakesh, connives with the French, pacifying rebellious tribes in exchange for power and privileges.

1923 La Mamounia Hotel opens.

1930–40s An independence movement centring on the Istiqlal Party emerges in Fez. Growing unrest is met with repression.

1953 El Glaoui and 300 allies convene in Marrakesh to draw up a proposal to replace the legitimate monarch (Sultan Mohammed Ben Youssef, later Mohammed V) with the elderly Ben Arafa. The true sultan and his family are exiled to Madagascar.

1955 Mohammed V is restored to the throne.

INDEPENDENCE

1956 France grants Independence. Mohammed V changes 'sultan' to 'king'.

1961 Accession of Hassan II.

1963–77 King Hassan survives the first of five different plots against him, the most serious of which are led by the army.

1969 *The Marrakesh Express* is released by Crosby, Stills & Nash. By now Morocco, Marrakesh in particular, is a stop on the hippie trail.

1975 The Green March: 350,000 unarmed Moroccans claim the Spanish (Western) Sahara for Morocco.

MODERN TIMES

1999 Hassan II dies. His son and successor, Mohammed VI, embarks on a programme of increased democratisation. He frees many political prisoners and improves women's rights.

2001 Marrakesh's International Film Festival is inaugurated.

2002 Mohammed VI marries. A son is born the following year.

2003 Terrorist bomb attacks in Casablanca kill 45 people.

2007 Third airport terminal in Marrakesh started; set to open in 2012.

2008 Saad Housseini is given 15 years for his part in the 2003 bombings.

2009 Apparent al-Qaeda leader in Morocco, Abdelkader Belliraj, is imprisoned for life.

Above from far left: an engraving of Marrakesh from 1836; a French Minister is presented at the Moroccan court in 1909.

Above: Sultan Abdelaziz's profligate spending bankrupted Morocco; King Hassan II was a highly autocratic leader; the national flag of Morocco.

WALKS AND TOURS

1

KOUTOUBIA MOSQUE AND JEMAA EL FNA

Like different sides of the same coin – one sacred, one profane – the Koutoubia Mosque and the Jemaa el Fna together encapsulate Marrakesh. They lie a short distance apart on either side of Place de Foucauld.

DISTANCE 1km (½ mile)

TIME 3 hours

START Koutoubia Mosque

END Jemaa el Fna

POINTS TO NOTE

This route is best done late in the day, when the Koutoubia glows in the evening sun, locals come to stroll in the Koutoubia Gardens, and activity on the Jemaa el Fna, which is comparatively low-key during the day, starts to build up.

This is not so much an itinerary linking two of the city's main sights as an immersion in the exhilarating atmosphere of Marrakesh. It is ideal for your first evening in the city.

KOUTOUBIA MOSQUE

The **Koutoubia Mosque** ❶ (Mosquée de la Koutoubia) is one of the icons of Marrakesh. Its lovely ochre-coloured minaret rises like a beacon from **Place de Foucauld**, marking the point in the Old Town where the long hike to

Calèche Rides
Place de Foucauld is the main departure point for calèche (carriage) rides (although you will also find ranks outside the big hotels). For information on prices and routes, see p.64.

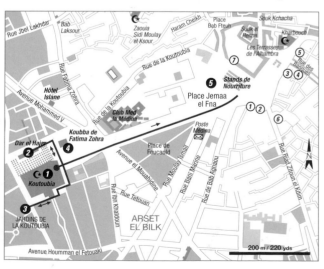

Guéliz, the New Town, begins *(see p.54)*. The interior is closed to non-Muslims, as it is a working mosque, but its exterior is worth a closer look.

The Booksellers' Mosque

Begun by the Almohad sultan Abdel Moumin in 1158 and completed by Yacoub el Mansour, the Koutoubia, or Booksellers' Mosque, is thought to be named after the scribes and Koran sellers who once plied their trade in the vicinity. It was not the Almohads' first attempt: excavations on the northern side of the complex have revealed bricked-up arches and the foundations of columns to support the roof of an earlier version, which may have been abandoned when it was discovered that it was not correctly aligned with Mecca.

Two sections of an earlier mosque, the **Dar el Hajar** ❷ (House of Stone), have also been exposed and can be viewed below the white frames on the forecourt.

The Minaret

The Koutoubia's **minaret** was the prototype for two other minarets in the Almohad Empire, the Tour Hassan in Rabat and the Giralda in Seville. It is nearly 70m (230ft) tall and follows the typical Almohad proportions of 1:5 (the height being five times the width). The exterior of the tower is decorated with stone tracery, each side displaying a different pattern. Originally, the unadorned stone would have been covered in plaster and decorated: bands of this decoration can still be seen near the top of the tower.

Above from far left: the Avenue Mohammed V leads from Place de Foucauld to Guéliz, the New Town; the Koutoubia's minaret in silhouette; a sunlit wall.

Below left: the Koutoubia's minaret.

The Almohads

The Almohads, or al-Muwahhidun as they were originally called, conquered Marrakesh in 1147. Bursting out of their tribal base in the N'fis Valley in the Atlas *(see pp.94–5)*, they descended upon the city, ousting the Almoravids, who had grown decadent after 90 years in power. From there they quickly spread north and east, and within a year they controlled the whole of Morocco. Eventually their empire stretched from Castile to Tripoli.

The greatest Almohad was Yacoub el Mansour ('the Victorious', 1184–99), whose reign saw a golden age in medicine, industry, architecture and the arts. However, as with the Almoravids, decline came within a century of seizing power. By 1230 the sultan was reduced to accepting 12,000 Christian cavalrymen from King Ferdinand of Castile and Leon in order to retake Marrakesh from local dissidents. In 1248 the Almohads were defeated by the Merenids, another Berber tribe, who established their capital in Fez.

Food and Drink 🍴

There are numerous places to eat on the square, and the following includes enough recommendations to cover several return visits. The first three are cafés; the remainder restaurants.

① CAFE LE GRAND BALCON

Drink in the views while lingering over a Coke or Fanta on this huge L-shaped terrace. The drinks, which must be bought at the counter as you walk on to the terrace, are relatively expensive, but this place really does provide the best vista.

② CAFE CTM

This is the café-terrace (for drinks only) of the long-established budget hotel of the same name. It is quieter than the neighbouring Café le Grand Balcon, but it also offers good views of the spectacle below.

③ CAFE DE FRANCE

This can't be missed due to its distinctive Coca-Cola-emblazoned awnings, even so it is one of the best cafés on the square to sit and watch the goings-on.

④ LE MARRAKCHI

52 Rue des Banques; tel: 0524-44 33 77; noon–1am; $$$
If you want a more up-market experience than the more basic establishments described below, but still overlooking the square, with soft furnishings, candlelight, good Moroccan food and alcohol, this is the place to come. Wraparound windows offer views of the eastern leg of the square.

⑤ CHEGROUNI

Jemaa el Fna, near Rue des Banques; no phone; 6am–11pm; $
Basic it may be in appearance, but this long-established restaurant offers views over the eastern periphery of the square. Expect reasonable brochettes, *harira*, lamb chops, *kefta*, salads and yoghurt. The grills are better than the couscous or tajines. No alcohol.

⑥ TOUKBAL

8 Jemaa el Fna; tel: 024-4442262; 7am–midnight; $
This basic café-restaurant on the corner of the square is a great place to sit and watch the world go by amid a mix of locals and foreigners. Try the chicken tagine with preserved lemon, and don't miss the home-made yoghurt.

⑦ ARGANA

Jemaa el Fna; tel: 0524-44 53 50; 6am–11pm; $
This place serves perfectly good café food, and its views of the square are excellent. No alcohol.

Around the Mosque

Behind the mosque, the **Koutoubia Gardens** ❸ (Jardins de la Koutoubia) are a popular place for an early evening stroll. Close to the road is the white **Koubba of Fatima Zohra** ❹, the tomb of the daughter of a 17th-century holy man who was known for her compassion and named after the Prophet Mohammed's own daughter.

Across Avenue Mohammed V, the Islane Hotel's terrace restaurant offers a tempting view of the mosque and the animated evening scene. Unfortunately, it is a bit of a tourist trap, serving mediocre food. Instead, head east across Place de Foucauld to the Jemaa el Fna to eat.

JEMAA EL FNA

The Koutoubia may be a favourite place for *Marrakshis* to congregate in the early evening, but it is a mere backwater in comparison with the heaving sea of humanity on the **Jemaa el Fna** ❺.

Variously translated as the place of the dead, place of destruction, or, most appropriately perhaps, the place of the apocalypse, the Jemaa el Fna is one of Africa's great squares. Despite the huge numbers of tourists in Marrakesh, most of whom are drawn here at some point in the evening, it remains an intensely Moroccan place. The very heart of Marrakesh, it defines the city's role as a marketplace and crossroads, where trans-Saharan trade caravans transporting salt, gold, sugar, spices and slaves once came to rest, the merchants seeking company and entertainment after weeks of hard travelling.

The Entertainers

Today the camel trains are gone, but company and entertainment remain in abundance. Acrobats and storytellers draw the crowds, as do the *fakirs* – medicine-cum-holy men with cures for everything from impotence to possession by *djinn* (demons) plus charms to fend off the evil eye. Fortune-tellers are also plentiful, although you will be hard-pressed to find one who speaks English.

Tourists tend to be targeted by women offering henna tattoos *(see margin right)* and snake-charmers. Usually belonging to the Assioua brotherhood, a Sufi sect founded in the 15th century by the mystic healer Sidi ben Aissa, snake-charmers don't just perform for tourists. Both revered and feared for their powers, they have a steady business in ridding properties of poisonous snakes and scorpions.

You will always find at least one or two bands of *gnaoua* musicians. Distinguished by their cowrie-trimmed hats and waistcoats, these black musician-healers are believed to be descended from West African slaves brought to Morocco by the Saadians in the 16th century. Often their performances are fairly tame, but when the vibe and audience are right, their music will continue until dawn, the hypnotic rhythms of the *darbuka* beating a very African refrain.

A Ringside Seat

Cooking up a storm in the centre of the square are rows of food stalls. This is the place to sample sizzling merguez sausages, brochettes, bowls of *harira* (a hearty soup), snails in a cumin-flavoured liquor, and, for the more adventurous, sliced sheep's head, tripe, calves' feet and much more. Trade is brisk, standards of hygiene reasonably well policed, and, providing you keep track of the prices, your bill will be very low. Alternatively, there are several café-restaurants with terraces offering views over the mesmerising scene *(see Food and Drink 🍴 box, left)*. Any of these is a good place to start or end an evening on the square.

Above from far left: evening bustle on the Jemaa el Fna; one of the many food stalls.

Hennaed Hands

Traditionally, henna tattoos are applied to the hands and feet of brides and female wedding guests. The effect will last up to four weeks, depending on how long you leave the henna on before rinsing. Rather than have your hand painted in the square, where the henna is mixed with chemicals, ask your hotel for a recommendation.

Water-Sellers

Among the many colourful figures on the square are the *gerrab* (water-sellers; *pictured left*) with their tasselled hats, studded leather girdles and necklaces of polished brass cups. A cup of water from a *gerrab*'s goat-skin will cost a few dirhams, a photograph rather more.

Far left: a snake-charmer.

THE SOUKS AND
BEN YOUSSEF MADRASSA

Forming part of the medina, the souks of Marrakesh are among the finest in the Arab world. Located north of the Jemaa el Fna, they extend to the Ben Youssef Mosque and Madrassa, the latter being one of the city's top sights.

Guides

Gone are the days when anyone entering the souks would be mobbed by would-be guides pressing their services. This is a good thing, as the unrelenting pressure to engage a 'guide' has ruined many a holiday. If you would like to use a qualified guide, hire one through your hotel. Alternatively, in the early morning, from outside Club Med on Place de Foucauld, unofficial guides gather – these will charge low prices, but are likely to be intent on getting you to shop as much as possible.

DISTANCE 1.5km (1 mile)
TIME A half-day
START Café de France, Jemaa el Fna
END Jemaa el Fna
POINTS TO NOTE

This walk is best suited to the morning, when the souks are in full swing and the monuments are open. The souks are considerably quieter, and therefore less atmospheric, in the afternoon, and although the cool of the early evening unleashes a fresh burst of commercial activity, the monuments close by around 6 or 7pm.

Marrakesh's medina is divided into two halves that are separated by the Jemaa el Fna. To the south are the main buildings of the Alaouite Dynasty (1631 to the present day), including several palaces, the *mellah* (old Jewish ghetto) and the Kasbah (*see pp.44–8*). Spreading north of the square are the city's labyrinthine souks, the most dazzling in all of Morocco, plus several of the city's oldest monuments. These include the 16th-century Ben Youssef Madrassa, which was built by the Saadians and is not to be missed.

THE SOUKS

Begin at the **Café de France ❶** (easily identified by its Coca-Cola-emblazoned awnings) on the eastern side of the Jemaa el Fna (*see p.32*). With your back to the café take the small entrance immediately opposite: this will bring you to **Souk el Henna ❷** (where henna, nuts, dried fruit and pulses are sold), which leads to an arch of lacy stucco.

Souk Semmarine

Through here, **Souk Semmarine ❸**, the main artery of the souks, stretches north. This used to be the souk of the blacksmiths who dealt specifically with horses and donkeys, but is now a vivid corridor of consumerism. If you more or less keep to this, you won't get lost; if you wander at random, you almost certainly will, although this will bring its own pleasures and surprises. As Elias Canetti says in *Voices of Marrakesh*, 'You will find everything but find it many times over.'

Souk Semmarine includes some very up-market souvenir shops selling genuine antiques, towers of myriad-coloured carpets, and bags and *babouches* (slippers) of the finest calf- and goatskin. Pressure to buy is far lighter than it used

to be; some shopkeepers lay off the sales patter entirely, making browsing not only possible, but pleasurable and engrossing.

The Spice Souks

After about 500m/yds, look out for a busy right turn (signposted) into **Place des Epices ❹** (Place Rahba Kedima). This square is filled with stalls selling spices and traditional cosmetics and medicines, as well as straw hats and baskets piled high in the centre. In addition to the mountains of different spices, look out for *savon beldi* (local soap), a black, tar-like soap made from olives; baskets of henna leaves (plus tubes of ready-made paste); and antimony (kohl) to darken eye rims. The last is used to

Above from far left: mounds of aromatic spices; decorative plates; dried figs; light and shade in the souks.

Medina Know-How
- Dress respectfully.
- Keep to the right.
- Move to the right if you hear a vehicle, to allow it to go past.
- Be easy-going and stay cool.
- Don't linger in front of shops if you don't want to buy.
- Avoid bargaining if you don't really want to buy.
- Always ask anyone before you take their photograph.

Below: a traditional mint-tea pot; sweet pastries.

Love Potions

In Place des Epices, foreign visitors are thought to be mainly interested in the various aphrodisiacs on sale. The most notorious, Spanish Fly (used by the Marquis de Sade in the 18th century), was actually banned in Morocco in the 1990s.

Below: Place des Epices and, to the left, Café des Epices.

protect as well as to beautify: children's eyes are sometimes rimmed with kohl to ward off evil spirits, especially after birth or circumcision.

The traditional medicine stalls are worth a closer look, too. Among the simple remedies, such as cloves to alleviate toothache and cardamom for poor circulation, are giant gourds, animal parts, ostrich eggs and feathers that are used in magic spells or as talismans.

Overlooking the square (on the left as you enter it) is the terrace of **Café des Epices**, see ⑪①, an ideal spot to take in the scene. Just off the northern side of the square is the former slave market. Slaves were traded here until 1912, when the French closed down what little remained of the market.

Souk el Kebir and Souk Cherratine

Retracing your steps to the point where you turned into Place des Epices, continue a few metres north to a fork. Either route from here will eventually take you to the Ben Youssef Mosque and Madrassa on Place Ben Youssef. For the sake of simplicity our walk takes the right-hand route, **Souk el Kebir ❺**, which leads there more or less directly.

Continue north, where a tight maze of alleyways offers all sorts of diversions, from musical instruments to saddles. Try to keep heading towards the minaret and green-tiled roofs of the Ben Youssef Mosque. On the way you will pass the **Souk Cherratine ❻**, where leather from the tanneries *(see p.38)* is worked into pouffes, slippers and bags.

Souk des Babouches, Kissarias and Souk Haddadine

As a more interesting, but potentially more disorientating, alternative, you could take the left-hand route from the fork just north of Place des Epices, heading via **Souk Attarine**.

Such is the popularity of the soft Moroccan slippers *(babouches)* with pointy toes and turned-down backs that **Souk des Babouches** (Souk Smata) has expanded into several neighbouring alleyways. Embroidered, bejewelled, and in countless gorgeous colours, the slippers can be hard to resist.

Between Souk des Babouches and el Kebir is the **Kissaria**, devoted to high-quality textiles and luxury goods; it is a great place to find fine-quality kaftans, including tailor-made garments.

Food and Drink 🍴

① **CAFE DES EPICES**
Place des Epices; tel: 0524-39 17 70; 9am–8pm summer (6pm winter); $
This café has ground-floor and first-floor terraces; the latter is more stylish with divan seating and views over the square. It serves drinks, sandwiches, *kefta*, omelettes and salads. It can get crowded, so it is best to lunch early or late.

North of Souk des Babouches, close to the Ben Youssef Mosque, is **Souk Haddadine** (Souk des Ferronniers), the metalworkers' souk. This is one of the most industrious in the medina, where sparks fly and workers turn out wrought-iron grilles, chairs, table frames, lanterns and a huge range of other goods, to meet the demand made by trends in interior design.

PLACE BEN YOUSSEF

This square is the location of three of Marrakesh's main sights, the Ben Youssef Madrassa, Koubba el Baroudiyn and Museum of Marrakesh. Each has its own entrance charge, but you can buy a combined ticket, available from each sight. Note that the **Ben Youssef Mosque** is closed to non-Muslims.

BEN YOUSSEF MADRASSA

The largest of Morocco's historic *madrassas* (Koranic colleges), **Ben Youssef Madrassa** ❼ (Médersa Ben Youssef; daily 9am–6pm, until 7pm in winter; charge) was begun in the 14th century by the Merenids, the dynasty most active in building *madrassas*. It was expanded by the Saadian sultan Abdallah el Ghallib, who wanted it to be the largest, most splendid of its kind in Morocco, rivalling those of the religious establishment based in Fez.

As is usual in Islamic architecture, the *madrassa*'s plain exterior walls give no hint of the staggering ornamentation inside, where every surface is covered in cedar and stucco carvings and *zellige* (mosaic tiling). In keeping with Islamic prescripts, animate representations are absent; instead intricately executed floral and geometric motifs are repeated in mesmerising patterns, an effect intended to focus the mind on the infinite power and purpose of God.

Above from far left: Moroccan slippers; the Ben Youssef Madrassa; vivid silks; a corridor in the *madrassa*'s central courtyard.

The Layout of the Souks

Traditionally, the centre of any medina was the main mosque, also known as the Friday mosque. Clustered around the mosque would be the souks: closest of all would be the luxury trades and goods (candles, perfume and fine textiles), including the 'kissarias', smart arcades that could be locked at night. Dirty or smelly industries, such as the tanneries, were located on the medina's edge, in the direction of the prevailing wind and close to a running-water supply. Each industry had its quarter and each contributed to the benefit of the whole – one of the governing principles of the wider Islamic society.

Over the last decade or so in Marrakesh, the traditional division of goods and labour that was once so distinct has become blurred. Many traditional goods have made way for tourist-orientated bazaars, and the old artisan quarters are less well defined than they used to be. Some businesses are slowly relocating to the periphery of the medina, where transport links are better, or to industrial parks in the suburbs of the New Town. That said, Morocco's souks are still among the most authentic in the world and ranked alongside those of Aleppo, Damascus and Cairo.

The Chrob ou Chouf Fountain
A short distance up Rue Dour Saboun, just behind the Ben Youssef Mosque, is the 16th-century Chrob ou Chouf ('Drink and Look') Fountain. Like several other historic fountains, all in need of restoration, it is lavishly embellished with a finely carved cedar mantel. Other famous fountains include the Mouassine Fountain (see p.42) and the one next to the Bab Doukkala Mosque (see p.43).

Students' Quarters

The two-storey complex centres on a marble courtyard with a rectangular pool. Around the edge of the courtyard on both levels are the students' quarters, 132 cells that would have been shared; a few are distinguished by a cupboard, a niche for storing possessions or a carved window surround. The cells can be inspected (two have been furnished as they might have been at the time: one for a wealthy urban scholar, and one for a poor country student).

Prayer Hall

The prayer hall on the ground floor is divided with pillars of Carrara marble and has a magnificent cedar ceiling. It also has a carved stucco *mihrab* (niche indicating the direction of Mecca), depicting intertwining foliage, pine cones and Koranic verses, with traces of its original blue and red colouring intact.

KOUBBA EL BAROUDIYN

Before entering the Museum of Marrakesh next door to the *madrassa*,

The Tanneries

If you are feeling adventurous, consider heading east along Rue Souk el Fes (behind the Ben Youssef Madrassa) and then Rue Bab Debbarh to the tanneries. Along the way look out for *fondouks*, which line parts of the route; these old galleried inns, some several hundred years old, originally offered lodging for merchants and their animals.

Perhaps because they are out on a limb near Bab Debbarh, the tanneries are not such a feature on the tourist map as the famous tanneries of Fez; relatively few visitors venture out this far. Nonetheless, like a giant paintbox, the network of pits, in which the workers wade waist-deep, presents a scene that has barely changed in 1,000 years. Morocco has long been famous for its leather; at one time, whole European libraries were sent here to be morocco-bound. The overpowering smell emanates from the substance used to make the hides supple, a mix of pigeon droppings and animal urine; small bunches of mint are handed out to squeamish nose-holding visitors.

Right: the tanneries.

backtrack to the **Koubba el Baroudiyn** ❽ (daily 9am–7pm, until 6pm in winter; charge), opposite the mosque. The importance of this simple two-storey sandstone structure, the one Almoravid building left in Marrakesh, lies in its seminal role in the development of Hispano-Mauresque architecture. The motifs and style that you see here – the stepped battlements, the keyhole arches, the carvings inside the dome – have been repeated and elaborated through eight centuries of North African architecture.

You will need to climb down to inspect the structure as it lies below present-day street level. Excavations have revealed the remains of a cistern, latrines and fountains, suggesting that the *koubba* formed the centre of an ablutions area for the nearby mosque, a far earlier incarnation of the 19th-century Ben Youssef Mosque that you see today.

MUSEUM OF MARRAKESH

The **Museum of Marrakesh** ❾ (Musée de Marrakech; daily 9am–6.30pm; charge) is housed in the Mnebhi Palace, the grand late 19th-century residence of Mehdi Mnebhi, a minister of Moulay Abdelaziz, the sultan whose profligate spending bankrupted the treasury and paved the way for European colonisation. The palace later became a property of Thami el Glaoui, the self-styled Pasha of Marrakesh *(see also p.85)*, and then passed into state hands when Morocco gained independence in 1956.

The building was restored and turned into a museum by the late

Omar Benjelloun, a wealthy entrepreneur whose foundation also restored the Koubba el Baroudiyn.

Moroccan Arts and Crafts

It is a splendid setting for a permanent collection of Moroccan arts and crafts, including jewellery, metalwork and carpets from the Anti-Atlas region, textiles from Fez and Tetouan, and ceramics from Fez and Safi, places that are famous for such products to this day.

The magnificent copper lantern over the central courtyard is 5m (16ft) in diameter and weighs 1,200kg (over one ton). You'll also find coins and calligraphy from across the Islamic world, as well as changing exhibitions by local and international artists. Items are displayed in the side rooms off the central courtyard, and also in the old hammam, an intimate domed complex studded with star-shaped skylights.

The courtyard café offers drinks and snacks, but a better bet for lunch is **Chez Abdelhay Frere Rachid**, see ⑪②, behind Ben Youssef Mosque (follow the road round the mosque, passing the Koubba el Baroudiyn).

Retrace your steps to the Jemaa el Fna – back along Souk el Kebir and Souk Semmarine is quickest; if lost, ask a shopkeeper to point the way.

Above from far left: arabesque in the *madrassa*; corridor in the Museum of Marrakesh; door handle; copper lantern above the museum's central courtyard.

The Almoravids
Although Marrakesh was the capital of the Almoravids (1060–1147), the only remaining structures of the great dynasty, whose empire stretched from Valencia to Senegal and from Morocco to Algiers, are the Koubba el Baroudiyn *(pictured)* and small sections of the city walls. The Almohads *(see p.31)* wiped out the rest.

Food and Drink 🍴
② CHEZ ABDELHAY FRERE RACHID
Behind the Ben Youssef Mosque; no phone; $
A clean, friendly and inexpensive spot for a tasty mixed grill comprising brochettes, lamb cutlets and *kefta* with egg, accompanied by salad, olives, fresh bread and soft drinks. In sunny weather a handful of trestle tables are set up outside.

3

THE MOUASSINE QUARTER

This walk covers the area to the west of the main souks. It takes in the dyers' quarter, the beautifully restored Dar Cherifa, and the palace of a powerful Atlas chief who colluded with the French during the Protectorate.

DISTANCE 2km (1¼ miles)
TIME A half-day
START Jemaa el Fna
END Koutoubia Mosque
POINTS TO NOTE
If time is limited you could pick up this route from Place Ben Youssef (see p.37), by heading west along Souk des Teinturiers to the Mouassine Mosque and Fountain.

Bijoux Boutiques
Bab Fteuh is flanked by shops selling cheap shoes, clothes and hardware. However, on the right side of the square as you enter is Akbar Delights (45 Place Bab Fteuh), specialising in high-quality textiles from Kashmir. Other individual shops are Beldi, 9–11 Souikat Laksour (just inside Bab Fteuh), 57 Al Kawtar, Rue Laksour (see margin p.21) and Kif Kif and Kulchi, at the end of Rue el Ksour (signposted off Souikat Laksour). Both offer chic clothing with an East-West bent.

The area northwest of the Jemaa el Fna is slightly different in character from the rest of the old city. More affluent and calmer, it has several up-market riads and restaurants, and a bohemian-chic vibe.

STARTING OFF

From the Jemaa el Fna *(see p.32)* take the route to the left of Café Argana as you face it, passing a plant market on your left, to reach **Place Bab Fteuh** ❶, a broad area full of life. Although the actual gate *(bab)* no longer exists, the spot retains the bustle of an entrance point.

On the left at the back of the square, beyond a no-entry sign for vehicles,

Souikat Laksour leads north, a sunnier and more open passage into the souks than shadowy Rue Semmarine on the eastern side of the Jemaa el Fna. It is also a quieter route, and its shops tend to be more individual than the twinkling bazaars in the main souks. Several contemporary design shops, boutiques and antiques shops have sprung up, especially in the area known as El Ksour between the Mouassine Mosque and Bab Laksour.

To explore this quarter, divert left at Bazaar Chichoua, pass through a white arch and walk along Rue el Ksour *(see margin, left)*.

MOUASSINE MOSQUE

Back on the main drag north, proceed for about 300m/yds until the route widens in front of the **Mouassine Mosque** ❷ (Mosquée Mouassine; closed to non-Muslims).

Built by the Saadian sultan Abdellah el Ghalib in 1562, it is considered to be one of the most impressive mosques in the medina: unfortunately, none of its splendour can be appreciated from its exterior, which is obscured by the many shops that cleave to its walls. Some of these have roof terraces with views into

the mosque's peaceful courtyards, but any invitations to climb up to a *terrasse panoramique* are likely to come at a price – some fairly heavy sales pressure.

Dar Cherifa

Just opposite the mosque, follow Derb Chorfa el Kebir (identified by a gold plaque reading 'Riad les Jardins de Mouassine') to **Dar Cherifa** ❸ (8 Derb Chorfa el Kebir; daily 8.30am–7pm; free), a magnificent house restored by Abdellatif Ait Ben Abdallah, a leading force in the authentic restoration of medina properties. You will need to knock to gain entry, but the welcome is warm. It holds exhibitions and concerts; its

Above from far left: antiques shop; mint; traditional teapots.

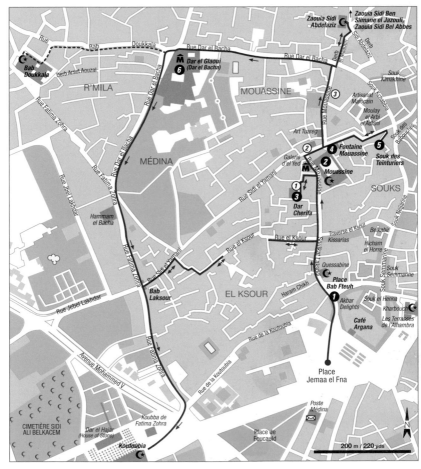

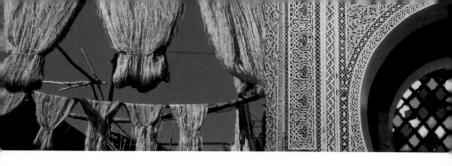

Clues to Medina Living

Wandering through the medina can be like wandering through a maze with high blank walls. Occasionally, an open door offers glimpses of its interior life, but, even so, dog-leg entrances mean that little is revealed. Yet clues can be gleaned, not just to daily activities but also to beliefs, superstitions and traditions.

Doors are often works of art, impressively studded, sometimes with a smaller inner door (for humans), leaving the larger for heavy loads or donkeys. The smaller door often makes the entrant bow their head, as if in humility. An obvious passage for *djinn* (demons), doors are often decorated with prophylactic symbols such as eyes, hands or geometric motifs. The knocker may be in the form of a hand (*khamsa*, meaning 'five'), representing the hand of Fatima, daughter of the Prophet, a symbol (which does not stem from scripture, as Islam does not use figurative symbolism) repeated many times in many different contexts (*see picture below*).

Stacks of logs usually mean the presence of a baker or hammam, often both, for it is common for these places to share a furnace; while children carrying trays covered by a cloth are taking home-made bread to be baked there. You may see older children spinning yarn to make braid for kaftans (the ends of the thread are tied to buildings on street corners). Local butchers offer a *tangier*, an earthenware urn that is filled with different types of meat then placed on the communal fire to make a tasty lunch. The sound of children chanting might indicate a *madrassa*, where

the Koran is recited by rote.

Stalls selling candles, nougat and other sweets usually indicate the presence of a shrine (*zaouia*) centred on the tomb of a holy man or woman. Although these are visited all year round, a large gathering of people is likely to indicate a *moussem* (religious festival).

café-cum-library, see ⑪①, is a great space to enjoy a peaceful drink, as is its rooftop terrace.

Mouassine Fountain

Back on the main drag, walk past the mosque and turn immediately right. The **Mouassine Fountain** ❹ (Fontaine Mouassine), a multi-bayed public fountain designed for animal as well as human use, dates from the 17th century. Although neglected, the fountain is one of several historic public fountains in the medina (*see margin, p.38*), reflecting the importance of managing and sharing water resources.

THE DYERS' SOUK

Just past the fountain, and worth a quick look, is the **Souk des Teinturiers** ❺ (Souk Sebbaghine), the dyers' souk. Sometimes the souk is indistinguishable from neighbouring alleyways, but on other days it is festooned with swathes of wool and silk, freshly dyed in vivid colours and hung out to dry above the street. A few dyers' workshops lie on either side; chemical dyes have replaced traditional plant dyes, but otherwise the process has barely changed for centuries.

If you continue east you will reach the Kissaria and Souk des Babouches, where you can pick up walk 2 (*see p.36*).

NORTH OF
THE MOUASSINE

Now double-back to the Mouassine Mosque to continue this walk. On the junction with Rue Mouassine is

Bougainvillea Café, see ①②, and further north, on the right-hand side of Rue Mouassine itself, is **Café Arabe**, see ①③, both decent options for lunch.

Shrine of Sidi Abdelaziz

The street continues north to the **Zaouia Sidi Abdelaziz**, one of seven *zaouias* (shrines centring on the tomb of a holy man or woman) that encircle the city. Two more – the **Zaouia Sidi Ben Slimane el Jazouli** and the **Zaouia Sidi Bel Abbes**, notable for its carved portal – lie further north. The *zaouias* are out of bounds to non-Muslims, and there are few reasons to venture further north, save for a few riads and restaurants that lie hidden in the residential maze.

Dar el Bacha

Shortly before you reach the Zaouia Sidi Abdelaziz, Rue Dar el Bacha leads west towards Bab Doukkala. On the way it passes the **Dar el Bacha ❻** (also known as Dar el Glaoui; daily 9am–noon and 3–6pm; charge). One of Marrakesh's most opulent buildings, it was restored and set up as a museum in 2007 by the late Patty Cadby Birch, an American collector of fine art and antiquities.

The property originally belonged to the Glaoui, overlords from the Atlas Mountains *(see p.85)*, who collaborated with the French during the Protectorate. The two brothers Thami and Madani Glaoui acquired vast wealth and influence: Thami was an acquaintance of Winston Churchill and attended the coronation of Elizabeth II. After Independence the Glaoui were disgraced and their properties seized by the state.

Return to the Koutoubia

From here you could make a detour west along Rue Bab Doukkala, which bustles with local life, to the **Bab Doukkala Mosque**, with its own fine fountain.

From the Dar el Bacha turn left and head south down Rue Dar el Bacha until you join Rue Fatima Zohra, which eventually reaches the Koutoubia. En route is the **Bab Laksour**; the shops on the streets inside (go left through the pretty arch and then right down Rue Laksour) are well worth dipping into *(see margin, p.40)*.

Food and Drink 🍴

① DAR CHERIFA
8 Derb Chorfa el Kebir; tel: 0524-42 64 63; 8.30am–7pm; $$
With a lovely peaceful setting and a homely atmosphere, this café serves juices, teas, salads, brochettes and omelettes, as well as one or two typical Moroccan dishes such as orange salad with cinnamon.

② BOUGAINVILLEA CAFE
33 Rue Mouassine; tel: 0524-44 11 11; 9am–11pm; $
This downstairs courtyard café is a bright and convenient spot (difficult to miss on the corner of the Mouassine Mosque) for a light lunch (pizza, panini, salads, omelettes, milkshakes, etc) or just a coffee or mint tea with pastries. No alcohol.

③ CAFE ARABE
84 Rue Mouassine; tel: 0524-42 97 28; www.cafearabe.com; 10am–midnight; $$
A café, restaurant and boutique hotel with a summer roof terrace and modern Moroccan/European fare such as salads and pasta. Serves brunch on Sunday.

Above from far left: the dyers' souk is hung with vibrant coloured wool and silk; the Bab Doukkala Mosque; a dyers' workshop.

Fondouks
Rue Mouassine, along with several other of the more important thoroughfares in the northern medina, is lined with ancient *fondouks*. These galleried lodging houses for traders and their animals are now given over to bazaars, storehouses or workshops, and sometimes used as sites in Marrakesh's thriving film-location business.

THE SOUTHERN MEDINA

This walk explores the area south of the Jemaa el Fna, where the sultans traditionally built their palaces. It visits the homes of two 19th-century viziers, and Maison Tiskiwin, the museum of a collector of Berber crafts.

Hazard Warning

The streets of the southern medina are relatively straight and easy to navigate. Cars move along them fairly slowly, but look out for speeding motorcycles. They zip past in all directions and make few allowances for pedestrians – especially dawdling foreigners.

DISTANCE 2.5km (1½ miles)
TIME A half-day
START Café de France, Jemaa el Fna
END Jemaa el Fna
POINTS TO NOTE

Make an early start if you want to visit all the sights on this walk, as Dar Si Said and El Bahia close for lunch at around noon. For a longer itinerary you could spend the afternoon visiting El Badi Palace and the Saadian Tombs, which are covered in Walk 5 *(see pp.49–53).*

Right: Café de France on the Jemaa el Fna.

The routes south of the Jemaa el Fna lead towards the palace area, Kasbah (stronghold of the city) and *mellah* (old Jewish quarter). The southern medina contains little in the way of souks, although there are some interesting individual shops on Rue Riad Zitoun el Jdid and a jewellery souk (mainly modern gold) off Place des Ferblantiers. The chief sights of the area are El Bahia Palace and two arts-and-crafts museums.

SETTING OFF

Start at **Café de France** ❶ *(see also p.32)* on the eastern side of the Jemaa el Fna, then take Rue des Banques, a straight residential street to the left of the café as you face it. After a couple of minutes' walk bear right at a T-junction marked by a small sign for Hôtel Mounir, and after a couple more minutes, pass through an arch with a no-entry sign for vehicles into **Rue Riad Zitoun el Jdid**. Up ahead you will see the minaret of a mosque; just before it, turn left through a red arch, proceed to the end and then turn right down **Derb Si Said** (*derb* means cul-de-sac), where signs point the way to the Dar Si Said Museum.

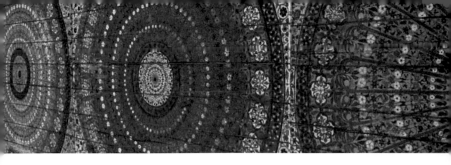

DAR SI SAID MUSEUM

Dar Si Said Museum ❷ (Derb Si Said; daily 9am–noon and 3–6pm; charge) is worth seeing for the setting alone. A typical 19th-century mansion, it was built for Si Said Ben Moussa, the brother of the sultan's grand vizier, Bou Ahmed, who lived in the nearby El Bahia Palace *(see* *p.47).* It now houses the Museum of Moroccan Arts, and is a superb repository of local craft. Through the entrance hall, where examples of traditional woodwork including carved doors, chests and *mashrabiyyah* (lattice-work windows) are displayed, a central courtyard leads to a series of rooms, each devoted to a traditional craft and their use in urban life.

Above from far left: tile at El Bahia Palace; intricate ceiling pattern.

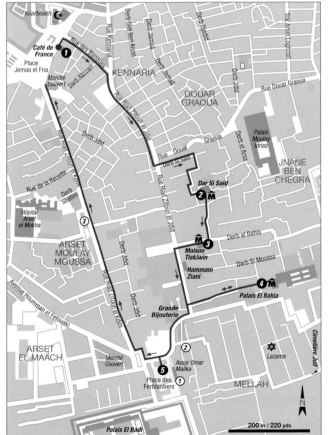

Garden Oases
The Dar Si Said Museum *(top)* and El Bahia Palace *(bottom)* have typical courtyard gardens. Their paths are laid out symmetrically, but the lush plants and trees intertwine and overarch, creating an enclosed and peaceful space that was ideal for private contemplation or the secret assignations of lovers.

Among the exhibits are finely engraved weaponry; items for personal care – combs, mirrors, kohl boxes – as well as leather buckets and clogs for visiting the hammam; a collection of musical instruments, including lutes and *rbab* (a single-string fiddle); and implements for cloth-making and leather-working.

Before continuing to the upper rooms you may want to pause in the garden, a leafy enclosure with fruit trees, a central pavilion and pool.

First Floor

The reception rooms on the first floor are more impressive, with elaborate *zellige* (mosaic tiling), stuccowork and woodwork. Look out for the exceptional ceiling of carved, painted and gilded wood. Items on display include a wedding chair, used for parading the bride and carrying her to her new home (traditionally her in-laws'); wooden toys and cradles; and a collection of kitchen implements, such as hammers for breaking blocks of sugar, leather bellows, kettles with in-built compartments for burning charcoal, and conical-lidded containers for holding bread. Look out for long-spouted vessels for pouring water over the hands of dinner guests, and incense-holders to waft the scent of amber or frankincense. To this day, incense and perfumed water are provided for the comfort of guests at weddings and other celebrations.

Second Floor

The second floor displays carpets and blankets from the Atlas Mountains. Their colours and decorative motifs – animist and astral symbols – offer clues to the specific region and tribe.

MAISON TISKIWIN

On leaving Dar Si Said, walk straight ahead and turn right. A little way along on the left is the **Maison Tiskiwin** ❸ (8 Derb el Bahia; daily 9.30am–12.30pm and 3–5.30pm; charge), a delightfully ramshackle old riad stuffed with arts and crafts collected by Bert Flint, a Dutch expatriate and anthropologist.

The collection – clothes, jewellery, headdresses, talismans, saddles and camel tack, carpets, domestic implements, weaponry and even a nomad's tent – traces the old Saharan trade routes from Marrakesh to Timbuktu in Mali. The displays are supported by detailed explanations in French and maps pinpointing the location of the many and various tribes represented.

The museum illustrates the rich melding of Arab, Berber and African influences and beliefs through trade, yet also highlights the subtle differences between regions and tribes.

EL BAHIA PALACE

Turn left out of the museum to return to Rue Riad Zitoun el Jdid. Turn left here, passing **Hammam Ziani**, a large hammam that is popular with young tourists. On the left, at the end of the street, is the **El Bahia Palace ❹** (Palais El Bahia; Rue Riad Zitoun el Jdid; Sat–Thur 8.45–11.45am and 2.45–5.45pm, Fri 8.45–11.30am and 3–5.45pm; charge), the palace of Bou Ahmed Ben Moussa, grand vizier to Sultan Abdelaziz, whose disastrous rule (he was just 14 when he acceded to the throne) and chronic overspending led to the foreign occupation of Morocco under Moulay Hassan in 1912.

Lavish Decoration

The complex of reception rooms, courtyards and gardens, which was seized by the royal family on the restoration of the monarchy, contains little in the way of furniture, but the decoration is lavish, with *zellige*, *zawwaga* (wood painted with floral patterns and arabesques) and carved stucco aplenty. This is particularly so in the first rooms, 'Le Petit Riad', where Bou Ahmed received official visitors. These rooms were also used by the French Resident General during the protectorate.

This area leads you through to La Petite Cour, with more rooms, and then La Grande Cour, on the left-hand side of which is the garden, and Le Grand Riad (1866–7), which was

The Mellah

The former Jewish quarter in Moroccan medinas is known as the *mellah*, a word that means 'salt' and is thought to allude to the Jews' domination of the salt trade in the 16th century, and in particular to their job of draining and salting the heads of decapitated rebels before they were impaled on the gates of a city. The *mellah* was normally located close to the royal palace to benefit from royal protection (on payment of a special tax). Marrakesh's *mellah* still contains vestiges of its once-sizeable Jewish community, including a functioning synagogue, occasional Hebrew signs and a large Jewish cemetery on the quarter's eastern side. Traditionally, the city's goldsmiths were Jewish, and, to this day, one of the main gold souks is situated off Place des Ferblantiers, on the *mellah*'s western edge.

Above from left:
gold belts at the
Grande Bijouterie;
El Badi Palace.

Buying Gold
The price of gold
jewellery is governed
by current gold
prices, which are
posted in the shops,
plus extra for the
work. Negotiate
on this basis.

the original palace belonging to Si Moussa, Bou Ahmed's father, and the quarters of Lalla Zineb, Bou Ahmed's first wife.

The Moroccan royal family still use the palace and make it available to celebrity guests: in 2002 Mohammed VI famously hosted a party here to celebrate the 33rd birthday of rap star P. Diddy, then known as Puff Daddy.

The Mellah

Behind the palace stretches the *mellah*, the old Jewish quarter, now home to just a few Jewish families, but with a definite Jewish character, with features such as Stars of David on the doors *(see box on p.47)*.

PLACE DES FERBLANTIERS

From the gates of El Bahia, go straight ahead and then make a dog-leg round to the left into pedestrianised **Place des Ferblantiers ⑤** on the edge of the *mellah*, passing into the adjacent square for the *ferblantiers* (metalsmiths) proper. En route you will pass the **Grande Bijouterie**, an arcade of goldsmiths crammed with 24-carat gold jewellery, such as heavy gold belts, filigree earrings and bracelets, a full set of which is traditionally given to a woman by her husband on marriage (rural brides are more likely to wear silver). Until recent changes in family law, such gold was sometimes all that a woman was entitled to take as a divorce settlement.

If you would like to visit El Badi Palace followed by the Saadian Tombs *(see Walk 5, pp.49–53)*, pass through the arch on the south side of the square and turn right alongside the walls of the palace to the ticket office.

Or, if you would prefer to stop for lunch, Place des Ferblantiers has several possibilities, including **Kosybar**, see ⑪①, and **Le Tanjia**, see ⑪②, as well as sandwich shops and brochette stands.

Afterwards, browse through the shops on and around Place des Ferblantiers. The square's huge range of ornate brass lanterns lure many buyers.

From Place des Ferblantiers you can return to the Jemaa el Fna along Rue Riad Zitoun el Kdim, a straightforward route. If you haven't yet eaten, the **Earth Café**, see ⑪③, at the far end, just by the square, does a tasty tajine at rock-bottom prices.

Food and Drink 🍴

① KOSYBAR

44 Place des Ferblantiers; tel: 0524-38 03 24; noon–1am; $$$
Lunch options here include well-made pasta and risotto, sushi and Moroccan classics with a modern twist. Has a good choice of alcoholic drinks, but you can just have a coffee or tea. Offers excellent views over Place des Ferblantiers and of the neighbouring storks from its terrace and several atmospheric bars.

② LE TANJIA

14 Derb Jdid, between El Bahia Palace and Place des Ferblantiers; tel: 0524-38 38 36; noon–3pm and 8pm–midnight; $$
Le Tanjiya's opulent interior, filled with divans and low tables, tends to fill with groups, but the Moroccan food remains good. Expect classic dishes such as *pastilla* and some of the more luxurious tajines (such as beef with hard-boiled eggs and almonds, and lamb with quinces). Service is variable and belly dancers sometimes make an appearance, but the terrace is lovely at dusk.

③ EARTH CAFE

2 Derb Zawak, Riad Zitoun el Kedim; tel: 661-289 409; $
This is something different in Marrakesh: a 'vegetarian vegan' café serving deliciously different dishes amid the jewel-coloured walls of a narrow courtyard. Expect dishes such as filo stuffed with pepper, courgette and ricotta, or with spinach, pumpkin and goat's cheese in an orange confit sauce.

EL BADI PALACE AND THE SAADIAN TOMBS

This walk, also in the southern half of the medina, visits the ruined palace of the Saadians and their hidden cemetery. Afterwards it stops for lunch in the kasbah area and suggests some postprandial pampering.

The Saadian Tombs are one of Marrakesh's top sights, and are all the more enchanting for their secluded setting in the shadow of the Kasbah Mosque. If you don't have time to do the whole of this route, a visit to the tombs should take precedence over El Badi.

SETTING OFF

From the Jemaa el Fna *(see p.32)* take Rue Riad Zitoun el Kdim to Place des Ferblantiers, a straightforward 10-minute walk. Cross the square, pass through the archway on the southern side, turn right and walk alongside the walls of El Badi Palace to the ticket booth and entrance.

EL BADI PALACE

El Badi Palace ❶ (Palais El Badi; Place des Ferblantiers; daily 8.30am–noon and 2.30–6pm; charge, plus extra to see the *minbar* of the Koutoubia Mosque) means 'the incomparable palace', but the ruined complex is more remarkable for its size than for its splendour. Enclosed by massive crumbling walls, topped by precarious-looking storks' nests, El Badi was built

DISTANCE 2.5km (1½ miles)
TIME A half-day, or a full day if you want to spend the afternoon being pampered.
START Jemaa el Fna
END Rue de la Kasbah
POINTS TO NOTE

The Saadian Tombs can get busy by mid-morning, so to avoid the bottlenecks make an early start. This tour can be combined with Walk 4, but as the heat and hassle of Marrakesh can kill the desire for too much sight-seeing, lunch followed by an afternoon in a spa is likely to be a more tempting option. If you want to have lunch and a swim in the Hotel Les Borjs de la Kasbah *(see p.52)*, take your swimming costume.

Views from El Badi
It is worth climbing up on to the great walls of El Badi (access on the northern side), from where there are lovely views over the medina's rooftops, the minaret of the Kasbah Mosque and, in winter, the Atlas Mountains.

by the great Saadian sultan El Mansour in the 16th century. It was financed by ransom money extracted from Portuguese nobles captured during battles, gold from the newly captured Songhai empire and profits from sugar production in the Souss Valley. According to contemporary accounts, El Mansour traded the

Above from left: horsemanship at a fantasia *(see below)*; the Kasbah Mosque's minaret; the Hall of Twelve Columns in the Saadian Tombs; the tomb complex, set around a garden.

sugar for Carrara marble, pound for pound, and imported the furnishings from China.

The palace took 25 years to build and was famously beautiful, its pavilions, towers and galleries impressing many a foreign ambassador. Sadly, however, it was short-lived: in 1683, Moulay Ismail, the second sultan of the current Alaouite dynasty, destroyed the palace, stripping its marble to furnish his own vast palace in Meknes, the new imperial capital.

Small patches of dusty *zellige* (mosaic tiling) can be seen here and there, but the most notable features today are the vast central courtyard and what remains of its once-famous sunken gardens that were ingeniously irrigated by pools fed by meltwater from the Atlas Mountains.

The Koutoubia's Minbar

Perhaps to draw more visitors to this rather bleak ruin, the **minbar** (moveable pulpit from which the imam leads the prayers and delivers sermons) of

Evening Entertainment
El Badi Palace impresses with its size, but is best appreciated as a venue for evening entertainment. Concerts – from rock to classical – are regularly held here, and in June it is the setting for a folklore festival. One of the highlights of the festival is a nightly fantasia – a dramatic display of horsemanship in which participants gallop towards each other, firing their muskets into the air. For details of events at El Badi look in *Couleurs Marrakech* (www.couleurs-marrakech.com, a free monthly listings booklet found in hotel lobbies and at the tourist office.

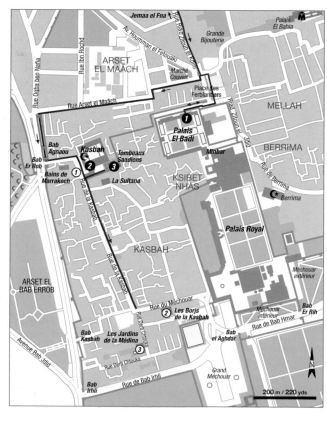

the Koutoubia Mosque *(see p.30)* is housed in a pavilion on the southwest corner of the courtyard. Intricately crafted in Córdoba for the Almoravid forerunner of the current Koutoubia Mosque, it is a masterpiece of Islamic art that took Andalusian craftsmen eight years to complete. In use in the Koutoubia until 1962, it was wheeled out on Fridays; the imam ascended only to the middle step in submission to God and the Prophet Mohammed.

THE KASBAH

Leaving El Badi, retrace your route to Place des Ferblantiers and continue in a westerly direction along Rue Arset el Maâch. At the bottom of the street cut left through an arch, head through two further arches (you are now passing between the Kasbah's double walls) and then turn left, leaving the handsome city gate, Bab Agnaou *(see p.65)*, on your right. The route leads towards the **Kasbah Mosque ❷** (Mosquée de la Kasbah; closed to non-Muslims), which, like Bab Agnaou, was originally built by the Almohads and thus is contemporary with the Koutoubia Mosque *(see p.30)*. However, its minaret – although topped by three brass spheres like the Koutoubia – is modest by comparison, and the mosque has been remodelled several times.

The kasbah (pronounced 'ksiba') is the stronghold of an Arab city, and in Marrakesh it protects the seat of power – the Royal Palace (Palais Royal) and Dar el Makhzen (House of Government; *see p.65*).

The Saadian Tombs

As you turn right into the broad area in front of the Kasbah Mosque, where a few souvenir stalls have taken root, you will see a sign for the **Saadian Tombs ❸** (Tombeaux Saadiens; Rue de la Kasbah; 8.30–11.45am and 2.30–5.45pm; charge), the cemetery of the Saadian sultans and their entourages.

Accessed via a slender passage on the corner of the mosque, the tombs were sealed off by the tyrannical Moulay Ismail in the 17th century and were

New Faces

A long-lasting legacy of Saadian sultan El Mansour's imperialist adventures was the influx of black slaves from West Africa, which added a new component to Morocco's rich ethnic mix.

Below: an entrance to the Saadian Tombs.

The Saadians

When the Saadian dynasty burst on to the scene in the 16th century, Morocco was in a feeble state. Anarchy had taken hold during the Wattasid dynasty, and the Portuguese controlled several Atlantic ports. Rising up from the Draa valley, in southern Morocco, the Saadians united supporters in the name of jihad, first basing themselves in Taroudant and then, in 1525, from their seat in Marrakesh. They were the first Arab – rather than Berber – dynasty to seize power since the Idrissids in the 8th century.

Under Ahmed El Mansur el Dehbi, 'the Victorious and Golden', their imperialist ambitions turned south, particularly to the gold-rich Songhai empire on the banks of the Niger, conquered by El Mansour in 1591.

Above: treat yourself to some pampering at a hammam *(see also pp.24–5).*

Hammams

The Kasbah area has several up-market spas, some attached to riad-style hotels, where you can spend the afternoon being pampered. Visits should be booked. Expect to pay from about 150DH for a hammam including body scrub to 1,200DH for full-day packages including several treatments. *See also pp.24–5.*

LES BAINS DE MARRAKECH

2 Derb Sedra, Bab Agnaou, Kasbah; tel: 0524-38 14 28; www.lesbainsdemarrakech.com; daily 9am–8pm, closed Aug

This is Marrakesh's most sublime spa experience: floaty curtains, white divans scattered with rose petals and moody lighting create a suitably sensual setting for an extensive range of treatments. Book around two weeks ahead.

LES BORJS DE LA KASBAH

Rue du Méchouar (off the southern end of Rue de la Kasbah); tel: 0524-38 11 01; www.lesborjsdelakasbah.com; opening times depend on bookings

This small riad-style hotel has created a marble-clad hammam and a relaxing treatment area in a watchtower built into the walls. Come for a light lunch *(see Food and Drink ⑪ box, opposite)* followed by a massage or beauty treatment.

LES JARDINS DE LA MEDINA

21 Rue Derb Chtouka; tel: 0524-38 18 51; www.lesjardinsdelamedina.com; daily 8.30am–8.30pm

This smart riad at the southern end of the Kasbah has a small but well-run spa with massages, wraps, facials and packages, including treatments for men.

LA SULTANA

403 Rue de la Kasbah; tel: 0524-38 80 08; www.lasultanamarrakech.com; daily 10am–8pm

A plush riad with a very stylish spa attached.

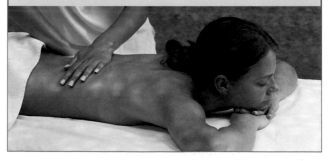

gradually forgotten until the early 20th century, when they were spotted on aerial photographs taken by the French.

Set around a garden, the complex contains 66 members of the Saadian dynasty plus the tombs of numerous retainers. The central mausoleum is known as the Hall of Twelve Columns; as you enter, the tomb of Ahmed el Mansour (1578–1603), who built El Badi Palace, is in the middle on the left, flanked by the tombs of his son and grandson. Fine *zellige* (mosaic tiling) work, intricately carved stucco and slender pillars supporting a spectacular cedar dome with the stalactite carving that is characteristic of Saadian architecture, provide a sumptuous yet elegant setting. To the left of the Hall of Twelve Columns is the prayer hall containing the graves of Alaouite princes from the 18th century.

On the other side of the cemetery another structure, with an ornate Andalusian-style entrance, contains the tombs of Mohammed ech Sheik, founder of the Saadians; Sultan Abdallah el Ghallib, who expanded the Ben Youssef Madrassa (see p.37); and Lala Messaouda, Ahmed El Mansour's mother.

A lunch option across the road from the tombs is **Nid' Cigogne**, see ⑪①.

Rue de la Kasbah

From the Saadian Tombs, **Rue de la Kasbah** leads south to Rue du Méchouar, named after the parade ground of the Royal Palace and Dar el Makhzen (see p.65). A lively north-south thoroughfare, Rue de la Kasbah is worth a

wander. At the start, near the tombs, look for the **Centre Artisanal** (a government-run shop selling fixed-price handicrafts). Even if you prefer to bargain in the souks, it's worth popping in to get an idea of prices beforehand.

Lunch and a Spa Option

If you fancy lunch by a pool, there are several nice riads in the Kasbah area, including **Les Borjs de la Kasbah** in Rue du Méchouar, see ⑪②, and, nearby, **Les Jardins de la Medina**, see ⑪③ (both have spas). There are also several kebab stands on Rue de la Kasbah. These can be good: a queue of locals will indicate if this is the case.

Having spent the morning sight-seeing, you may wish to reward yourself with an indulgent afternoon in a spa (see Hammams box, opposite).

Above from far left: La Sultana, a plush riad and spa; poolside at Les Borjs de la Kasbah; view of the Kasbah Mosque from La Sultana.

Food and Drink

① NID' CIGOGNE

60 Place des Tombeaux Saadiens; tel: 0524-38 20 92; 9am–9pm; $$
Serves salads, sandwiches, omelettes and basic couscous and tajines, but is best for its terrace views over the Kasbah Mosque and the storks' nests that crown the Kasbah's walls.

② LES BORJS DE LA KASBAH
Rue du Méchouar; tel: 0524-38 11 01; lunch 12.30–2pm, dinner 8–11pm; $$
You can order a simple lunch by the pool (swim included) or a more elaborate meal on the central patio in the adjacent restaurant. The chef prides himself on his well-executed modern French cuisine, but a few Moroccan options are always available.

③ LES JARDINS DE LA MEDINA
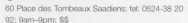
21 Derb Chtouka; tel: 0524-38 18 51; lunch noon–2.30pm, dinner 5.30–10.30pm; $$$
Worth a visit for the vast and varied Mediterranean buffet served by the pool from noon on Sunday. On other days there is a good-value set menu as well as à la carte. The pool is for residents only.

6 GUELIZ: THE NEW TOWN

Although lacking in sights, the New Town's wide boulevards, parks, good cafés and air-conditioned shops can make a refreshing change from the medina. This tour takes a morning stroll along and around its main artery, Avenue Mohammed V.

DISTANCE 3km (2 miles)
TIME A half day
START Koutoubia Mosque
END Place Abdel Moumen Ben Ali
POINTS TO NOTE

This walk, which includes opportunities for shopping, is best suited to the morning. If you want to extend it into the afternoon, you could also include the Majorelle Garden *(see pp.58–60)*, located a 10-minute walk from Place Abdel Moumen Ben Ali.

Below: the Eglise des Saints Martyrs.

At some point in your stay, you will most likely go to Guéliz, Marrakesh's new town, perhaps to book tickets at the railway station or Supratours office, visit a particular restaurant, or drop by the National Tourist Office. You may even be staying in Guéliz, as it has a plentiful supply of small- and medium-size hotels *(see p.113)*.

A Place Apart

Guéliz was laid out in the early 20th century by French architect Henri Prost. As with Morocco's other French-built cities, it was set well apart from the medina, in keeping with a decree of General Lyautey *(see p.57)*, the first Resident General. Although an arch colonialist, he believed the indigenous culture should be respected rather than erased. This approach led to the isolation of the medinas in the short term, but ultimately it ensured their long-term survival and preservation.

The French colonial influence, including striking examples of Art Deco, is still evident in the architecture more than 50 years after Independence, but it is steadily being edged out by that of the wealthy Gulf States, with their penchant for soaring marble lobbies, plate glass and air-conditioning.

THE MAIN ARTERY

Guéliz is divided by **Avenue Moham-med V**, a long broad road marked by the Koutoubia *(see p.30)* at one end and a small range of hills, the 'Guéliz', topped by the walls of an old French fort, at the other. In between, apartment and office blocks in the obligatory pink sandstone flank either side. The walk from the Koutoubia on Place de Foucauld to Place Abdel Moumen Ben Ali, the hub of the New Town, is a popular route for promenading *Marrakshis* in the early evening.

Bab Nkob

Begin the walk between the two halves of the city at the **Koutoubia ❶**. Leave

the medina by **Bab Nkob ❷**, a broad breach in the city walls rather than an actual gate, and head along the avenue.

Cyber Parc

On the left, just before Bab Nkob, is the **Cyber Parc**, a garden planted with olive, mimosa, acacia and fig trees, and with a café, auditorium and free open-air internet stations, a public initiative of Maroc Telecom and its global partners.

Catholic Church

Over the next big junction, **Place de la Liberté**, take the second left, Rue de Imam de Ali, down to a little Catholic church, **Eglise des Saints Martyrs**, built in the 1930s and now facing a modern mosque. To visit the church, which

Above from far left:
Place de la Liberté,
looking towards
the Guéliz hills; the
Cyber Parc.

Buses and Taxis

You can travel between Place de Foucauld and Place Abdel Moumen Ben Ali on the no. 1 bus, which is boarded from the first bus stand on Place de Foucauld (opposite the Koutoubia). A taxi costs about 20–30DH *(see p.108)*.

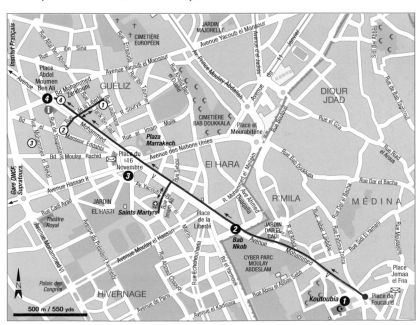

Cultural Concerns

French culture is alive and well at the Institut Français (tel: 0524-44 69 30; www.ifm.ma), located out on a limb on Route de Targa (the northern continuation of Avenue Mohammed V). The cultural institute runs a lively programme of films, dance, concerts and exhibitions, and is worth checking out. Details of forthcoming events can be found in *Couleurs Marrakech*, a free listings booklet that can be picked up in hotels, restaurants and other venues.

draws a mainly West African congregation, knock on the door to the left of the main entrance.

Place du 16 Novembre

Return to Mohammed V and head a little further on to **Place du 16 Novembre ❸**, which commemorates the day Mohammed V returned from exile in 1955, and is dominated by the main post office. On the opposite side of this intersection is **Plaza Marrakech**, a shopping mall full of fast-food outlets and shops selling up-market womenswear, home decor and sportswear.

Luxury on Liberté

A few blocks further north, Mohammed V crosses **Rue de la Liberté**, a smart street harbouring several of the

city's more exclusive shops. On the right-hand side of the junction you will notice small groups of waiting women – casual maids hoping, often in vain, to be hired for the day.

Close to here is a gallery showcasing a genius in Moroccan contemporary design, Yahya Création (61 Rue de Yougoslavie, Shop 49–50), with lamps designed by Yahya that take Moroccan light-making to another level. Rue de la Liberté's shops display a more restrained side to Moroccan design than the exuberant bazaars of the medina. Along the right leg, **Scènes du Lin** (no. 70) sells cushions, throws, tablecloths and glassware, and wonderful fabrics by the metre. Close by are several up-market jewellers and *traiteurs*; and the exclusive **Secrets de**

Food and Drink 🍴

① CAFE DU LIVRE
44 Rue Tarik ibn Ziad; tel: 0524-43 21 49; 9.30am–9pm, closed Sun; $$
This first-floor café-cum-bookshop is set back from the street alongside Hotel Toulousain. Leaf through design magazines and second-hand novels while tucking into home-made cakes, coffee, hot chocolate or mint tea, or choose something from the well-priced menu (soups, mushroom risotto, salads, sandwiches, tapas). It has modern art on the walls, a fire in winter and cocktails in the early evening.

② KECHMARA
3 Rue de la Liberté; tel: 0524-42 25 32; www.kechmara.ma; 7.30am–midnight, food served noon–11pm; $$
Sleek and chic, with Panton chairs and good-value set menus featuring modern European dishes with Moroccan influences, WiFi and cocktails. There is live jazz Wednesday to Friday evenings and DJs till late at weekends. It is located on the left-hand leg of Rue de la Liberté (far end), as you walk north along Avenue Mohammed V.

③ AMANDINE
17 Rue Mohammed el Bekal; tel: 0524-44 95 88; 7am–9pm; $
A favourite patisserie-cum-ice-cream parlour with a tiled interior and potted palms. It is ideal for morning coffee or afternoon tea with choice French cakes or sticky oriental sweets. Closed at lunchtime. No alcohol.

④ CAFE LES NEGOCIANTS
Place Abdel Moumen Ben Ali; 0524-43 57 82; 6am–11pm; $
Secure a table (not always easy) on the large wrap-around terrace and watch the passing scene over orange juice, coffee and croissants or a simple mint tea. Highly professional old-school waiters. No alcohol.

Marrakech spa (no. 62). One of the city's best commercial art galleries, **Matisse** (www.matisse-art gallery.com) is at no. 61.

Liberté's left leg offers more luxury shops, including, on the corner with Mohammed V, **Place Vendôme** (leather bags and saddles) and, next door, the Belgian chocolate shop, **Jeff de Bruges** (no. 17). Further along the street, **L'Orientaliste** (nos 11 and 15) sells hefty antique furniture and over-sized ceramics.

Refreshment Options

For a late breakfast or early lunch in the area, try **Café du Livre**, see ⑪①, on Rue Tarik ibn Ziad. **Kechmara**, see ⑪②, is a stylish restaurant-bar on Rue de la Liberté. If you just want a coffee and a sit down, **Amandine**, see ⑪③, on Rue Mohammed el Bekkal, is one of the best patisseries in town.

Centre Point

Return to Mohammed V and head a little further north to the busy **Place Abdel Moumen Ben Ali ❹**, where the terrace of **Café les Négociants**, see ⑪④, is a well-loved vantage point. Also here is the **National Tourist Office** (Office National de Tourisme; *see p.107*).

The only reasons for venturing further north are to book tickets at the Supratours office or the railway station (both on Avenue Hassan II), or to visit the Majorelle Garden *(see p.58)*, a 15-minute walk away on Boulevard Mohammed Zerktouni and Avenue Yacoub el Mansour.

Above from far left: leather shop on Rue de la Liberté; Café les Négociants; alfresco drinks at the café; the National Tourist Office.

Below: General Lyautey.

The French Protectorate

In the 'last scramble for Africa', the great land grab by European powers at the end of the 19th century, Morocco was one of the last countries to be claimed. An independent Islamic country for over 1,000 years, with a strong tribal structure and dynastic government, it wasn't considered an easy country to colonise. However, French loans to the weak and profligate Sultan Abdelaziz (1894–1908) led to increasing European encroachment, and in 1912 the Treaty of Fez made Morocco a 'protectorate' of Spain and France. Spain gained the poorer north and the Spanish Sahara, and France gained 'useful Morocco', as General Lyautey, the first Resident General, liked to call it. While Spain was a neglectful colonial master, France set about modernising its territory, developing agriculture and industry and building roads, ports and a railway.

7

MAJORELLE GARDEN AND THE PALMERAIE

This tour visits a dramatic garden designed in the 1920s by the painter Jacques Majorelle, then continues to the Palmeraie, an ancient date plantation that has become a 'des res' for numerous celebrities.

DISTANCE 6km (3¾ miles)
TIME A half-day or longer if you want to play golf or ride at the Palmeraie Golf Palace
START Majorelle Garden
END Palmeraie Golf Palace
POINTS TO NOTE
This tour is best undertaken mid-afternoon, when the heat and light have mellowed.

The Majorelle Garden is a straight-forward walk east from Place Abdel Moumen Ben Ali in Guéliz, but if you also wish to include the outlying Palmeraie you will need transport – a taxi or a calèche.

MAJORELLE GARDEN

The **Majorelle Garden** ❶ (Jardin Majorelle; Avenue Yacoub el Mansour; www.jardinmajorelle.com; summer

Below: details from the Majorelle Garden.

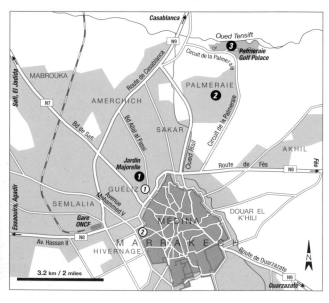

8am–6pm, winter until 5pm; admission charge plus an extra charge for the Museum of Islamic Arts) is one of the city's top attractions.

Jacques Majorelle

The garden was designed by the French painter Jacques Majorelle (1886–1962) in the 1920s and restored by Yves Saint Laurent and his partner Pierre Bergé during the 1980s. The son of the French furniture-maker Louis Majorelle, Jacques visited Marrakesh in 1917 to recuperate from an illness. He had come at the suggestion of General Lyautey, French Morocco's first Resident General and a family friend.

By this time the painter had already travelled widely in Egypt, but it was Marrakesh that held his fascination. First he used it as a springboard for forays into the Atlas Mountains and Sahara desert, then in 1924 he bought a plot of land on the edge of the French quarter and built Villa Bou Saf-Saf in the local style.

He later commissioned the architect Paul Sinclair to build a separate studio (now the Museum of Islamic Arts) in a neo-Mauresque style; it was the first structure in the garden to be painted cobalt blue, a colour Majorelle had been mesmerised by in the Atlas, where it is used extensively.

The garden took shape over a period of nearly 40 years, with plants sourced from all over the world. Although he was a painter, the garden is said to be Majorelle's greatest work, and he opened it to the public as early as 1947.

Sadly, he did not end his days here: following a car accident, he returned to France, and died soon afterwards.

The Garden

Spiky succulents and palms, towering bamboos and giant ferns are set off by brilliant cobalt-blue pavilions, terracotta paths and pots, and splashes of hibiscus and bougainvillea tumbling over walls and other verticals. The drenched colours and graphic shapes evoke a Gauguin painting; the shady pools and other water features add to the garden's elemental, faintly disturbing feel.

Museum of Islamic Arts

The **Museum of Islamic Arts** (Musée d'Art Islamique; extra charge) in Majorelle's former garden studio is currently undergoing refurbishment, but may have reopened by the time you read this. It is an attractive setting for a fine collection of jewellery, furniture, woodwork, textiles, weaponry and ceramics (with explanatory notes in English) from across the Islamic world, collected by Saint Laurent and

Above from far left: the Majorelle Garden and the Museum of Islamic Arts; a cobalt blue wall.

Below: spiky succulents in the garden.

Above from left: swimming pool at the Palmeraie Golf Palace; the Menara gardens and pavilion.

Camel Rides
The Palmeraie is dotted by clusters of brightly saddled camels, offering mini-safaris to any tourists who care to stop. If you fancy a *Lawrence of Arabia* experience among the palms, negotiate a price.

Below: riding school at the Palmeraie Golf Palace.

Bergé over the years. There are also a dozen or so of Majorelle's paintings of kasbahs in the Middle and High Atlas. On the wall in the last room that you come to is a poster advertising the 'Grand Atlas', one of several designed by Majorelle for a campaign to promote tourism in the 1920s.

Next to the museum is the courtyard **café**, see 🍴①, which offers drinks and light refreshments, and a small shop that sells a selection of tasteful gifts; or you can wander five minutes down the road to recommended local haunt **Café Glacier Snack Reda**, see 🍴②, a simple but tasty lunch choice.

THE PALMERAIE

The **Palmeraie** ❷, a wealthy area of palatial properties, lies off the Route de Fès on the northeast side of Marrakesh, about 5km (3 miles) from the centre or 3km (2 miles) from the Majorelle Garden.

According to legend, this ancient palm grove marks the camp of the invading Almohads in the 12th century and is the legacy of the soldiers' discarded date stones. This suggests a lush oasis, but the reality is a rather thin landscape of stooping palms (watered by ancient artesian wells), mud walls and dusty roads.

Nevertheless, a visit in the late afternoon, when the light softens the harshness of the landscape, is a pleasant prospect. Scattered among the mansions are several hotels and restaurants, including the opulent **Palmeraie Golf Palace** ❸ *(see p.113)*. Among its luxurious facilities are a superb golf course *(see p.23)*, stables where horses can be hired by the hour or half-day, and **Nikki Beach**, *(see p.123)*, all open to non-residents. From here take a taxi, calèche or bus back to your hotel.

Food and Drink 🍴

① MAJORELLE GARDEN
Avenue Yacoub el Mansour; tel: 0524-30 18 52; 8am–5pm; $$
The garden's secluded café has a pretty courtyard with wrought-iron chairs and parasols. You can order hot and cold drinks (including an extensive range of teas and fresh juices), brochettes, omelettes, soup and daily specials.

② CAFÉ GLACIER SNACK REDA
Avenue Yacoub el Mansour; no phone; 8am–10pm; $
A short walk from Majorelle Garden, this simple local favourite has outdoor seating and basic tasty grills, salads, etc. Try the chicken brochettes.

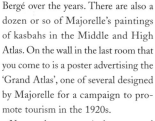

THE MENARA

*A gentle jaunt to the Menara is one of Marrakesh's classic calèche rides.
After a walk around the gardens, return via La Mamounia Hotel,
the former haunt of Winston Churchill.*

8

One of the attractions of the Menara gardens is the classic view of the central pavilion framed by the snow-capped Atlas, a scene that accounts for almost as many postcard sales as the Jemaa el Fna. However, this truly stunning vista is only possible on a clear winter or spring day (usually November–May), as in summer and autumn the mountains are not only snowless but also usually obscured by a dusty haze.

If conditions are right, the gardens are well worth a late-afternoon or even a sunset visit. To get here, hire a calèche at any of the calèche ranks: Place de Foucauld *(see p.30)* always has plenty. Be prepared to bargain, but you should pay around 150DH for the driver to wait and return.

DISTANCE 4.5km (2¾ miles)
TIME 2 hours
START Place de Foucauld
or another calèche station
END La Mamounia Hotel
POINTS TO NOTE

If you do not want to take a calèche or taxi to the Menara, you can walk here from the Bab Jdid, which is east of the Koutoubia, in about 20 minutes. Alternatively, you could get here by public bus (no. 11) from Place de Foucauld. The Menara is also a stop on the hop-on, hop-off sightseeing bus Marrakech Tour, on the 'Marrakech Monumental' route, beginning and ending in Guéliz.

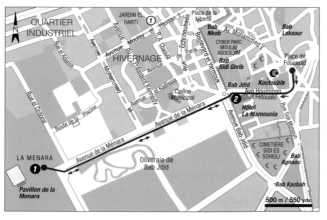

Menara Magic
The Menara's pavilion offers views not only of the Atlas but also of the great plain of Marrakesh, a sea of olive trees to the fore and the Koutoubia rising in the distance. Often the views are complemented by the sounds of music-making teenagers, who come here to sing, clap and beat *dabrouka* drums.

Above from left:
on duty at La
Mamounia Hotel;
early morning at
Bab Aghmat.

THE MENARA

The **Menara** ❶ (Avenue de la Menara; daily 5.30am–6.30pm; free) was established by the Almohads in the 12th century to provide agricultural produce for the sultan and for profit. In the 16th century the Saadians added a summer pavilion where the courtiers could catch the cooling mountain breezes, although this was remodelled by the Alaouite Sultan Abderrahmane in 1869.

Ascend the pavilion's staircase (entrance on the south side; charge) to see its painted ceiling and for views over the great square basin, measuring 800m (875yds) in perimeter and 2m (6ft) deep. Then stroll in the olive groves or enjoy a mint tea in the small café behind the seats on the far side of the pool.

LA MAMOUNIA HOTEL

You could end this tour by visiting **La Mamounia Hotel** ❷ for a drink or a

bite to eat – you will pass it on your return along Avenue Bab Jdid. This was Winston Churchill's choice when he was in town – he visited on several occasions during his retirement, as he liked to come here to paint. This is *the* Marrakesh hotel, and its revamp sees it retain its crown as Marrakesh's most glamorous place to stay. It has been beautifully renovated with a greater emphasis on traditional Moroccan decoration than the original Art Deco. The remaining pocket of pure Art Deco is the leather- and wood-panelled Le Bar Churchill. Its bars and restaurants (Le Pavillon de la Piscine is by the pool and Le Marocain is a traditional riad restaurant) are open to non-guests, so you can enjoy a taste of luxury even if you can't afford to stay here; dress smartly if you want to visit.

Alternatively, dip further into the Hivernage area, where cafés and ice-cream parlours are interspersed among the big hotels. The Kawkab Centre on Avenue Moulay el Hassan I has several interesting possibilities, including **Tanzania**, see ⑪①, a huge but hip restaurant-bar.

Ardent Fan
Winston Churchill
loved Marrakesh,
and especially La
Mamounia Hotel.
In 1943, after
the Casablanca
Conference, he
brought President
Roosevelt here.
'It is the most lovely
spot in the whole
world', he told the
president, as they
watched the sun
go down together.

Food and Drink

① TANZANIA

Kawkab Centre, Avenue Moulay el
Hassan I; tel: 0524-43 27 88; dinner
7.30pm–1am; $$$$
For an early evening cocktail, you
could try Tanzania, a vast, extravagant open-air restaurant-bar in the
Kawkab Centre. Live music (soul,
jazz, funk), for which it is known,
doesn't get going until 10.30pm.

TOUR OF THE GATES

*Marrakesh is encircled by some 16km (10 miles) of red sandstone
walls punctuated by a dozen gates. The best way to appreciate
their majesty is to take a 'tour des remparts' by calèche.*

One of the longer calèche rides, this
complete circuit proceeds clockwise
from **Place de Foucauld ❶**, pointing
out the more important gates. If you
prefer to sample a section of the fortifications rather than see the whole
thing, your calèche driver will probably
suggest you combine a tour of the leafy
Hivernage area *(see p.62)* with a trot by
the western walls to the Royal Palace.
It is a lovely trip in the evening, when
the gates and walls are illuminated.

DISTANCE 16km (10 miles)
TIME 2 hours
START Place de Foucauld
END Place de Foucauld, or
possibly your chosen restaurant
for the evening or your hotel
POINTS TO NOTE
This ride is likely to cost up to 250DH
(more with stops); be sure to negotiate
the fare before you set off *(see p.64)*.

Marrakesh the Red
'Fez is Europe but
closed; Marrakesh is
Africa, but open. Fez
is black, white and
grey; Marrakesh is
red.' John Gunther,
Inside Africa (1955).

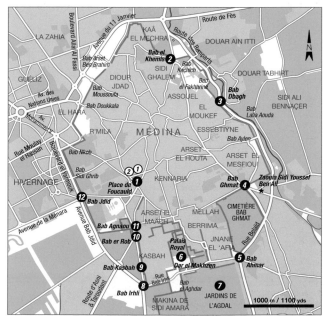

HISTORY OF THE WALLS

Although they have fallen and risen at various times in the city's history, the walls of Marrakesh were first laid out by the Almoravids as defence against the invading Almohads. Originally there were some 20 gates in all, but many are now bricked up or incorporated into dwellings, with only about half that number still functioning as entrance and exit points.

Your calèche driver will likely tell you the names of the more notable gates, but look out for (clockwise from north) **Bab el Khemis** ❷ (Thursday Gate – named after a Thursday market that has long taken place here) and **Bab Dbagh** ❸, both with finely carved façades, and **Bab Ghmat** ❹, through which the Almohads were able to capture the city in 1147, reputedly when starving Christian mercenaries flung open the portals. Just opposite is the **Zaouia Sidi Youssef Ben Ali**, a shrine to one of Marrakesh's 'seven saints'.

Keeping Cool
The walls and gates are pierced with holes, often crumbling these days and frequently home to nesting birds. These were not intended for weaponry, but are an ingenious type of air-conditioning system, allowing refreshing breezes to blow through.

Calèches

Calèches are one of the symbols of pleasure-loving Marrakesh. These lovely carriages, with their great folding hoods and brass lamps, are a pleasure to behold, and the clip-clop of hooves is undeniably romantic, especially on a warm summer night. Concern for the horses deters some tourists. In fact, the industry is better regulated than it used to be, and most of the animals are in good condition. The drivers are required to have two sets of horses, so that one can rest while the other is working, and the issuing of licences is dependent on horses undergoing regular veterinary inspections.

Calèches can be hailed for a short journey, much like taxis, although drivers don't like going into the narrower streets of the medina, where manoeuvring may be a problem. It is more common to hire one for an excursion – to add to the occasion – or for half a day to visit several sights.

The cost and duration should be agreed in advance, but expect to settle on around 50 percent more than the official rates posted inside the carriage. Calèche ranks are found on Place de Foucauld, between the Jemaa el Fna and the Koutoubia, and outside the larger hotels. The carriages can take up to five passengers, with one on top with the driver.

THE ROYAL PALACE

Skirting the cemetery, the route reaches the southern end of the medina and the **Bab Ahmar** ❺ (Red Gate), the entrance to the massive **Royal Palace** (Palais Royal) and **Dar el Makhzen** ❻ (House of Government). The external part of the complex comprises three linked *méchouars* (parade grounds), which held 22,000 soldiers, according to the 19th-century *Times* correspondent Walter Harris, who visited the palace in 1887. Today the palace is used mainly for state occasions (Mohammed VI has a smaller palace on Rue Sidi Mimoun, on the western side of the medina).

Opposite the palace are the **Agdal Gardens** ❼ (Jardins de l'Agdal), an agricultural estate established by the Almohads that still provides fruit for the royal household. Should you visit these during the day (they are a popular spot for picnics), you will find several pavilions and pools built by the Saadians.

THE WESTERN GATES

Returning north towards the Jemaa el Fna, the route goes through **Bab Irhli** ❽ and then alongside the Kasbah's **Bab Kasbah** ❾, and, after proceeding through the double portal of **Bab er Rob** ❿ *(see margin, right)*, then passes **Bab Agnaou** ⓫, with its beautifully carved concentric arches in blue-grey stone, which was built by the Almohads and remodelled in the 19th century.

From here the route returns to the Place de Foucauld, but you could ask to go via **Bab Jdid** ⓬ (the New Gate), where La Mamounia Hotel *(see p.62)* makes a suitably spectacular end to your tour.

Other up-market possibilities are **Les Jardins de la Koutoubia**, see ⓰①, or take a 10-minute walk through the Medina and eat at the marvellous **Le Foundouk**, see ⓰②. Alternatively, the Jemaa el Fna offers a host of inexpensive options *(see p.32)*.

Above from far left:
Bab Agnaou; detail on a calèche; Bab Dbagh; the Agdal Gardens.

Grapes of Wrath
Bab er Rob means Gate of the Grape, so named because it was the only gate through which grape juice could be brought, enabling the sultan to control the trade. It was also here, in 1308, that the Merenid Sultan Abou Thabit displayed the heads of 600 decapitated rebels.

Below left: doorway at the Royal Palace.

ESSAOUIRA

Marrakesh is intense and, in high summer, exceedingly hot. The fortified coastal town of Essaouira, 176km (110 miles) west, makes the ideal escape, soothing the senses with its mellow ambience and fresh sea breezes.

When to Go

Winter temperatures of about 20°C (68°F) make Essaouira a year-round destination, though heavy sea mists can descend in any season. Strong winds attract surfers and kite-boarders year-round, though the best conditions for these are at Sidi Kaouki, about 27km (16 miles) south, and Moulay Bouzerktoun, 20km (12 miles) north, where camper-van parks and makeshift cafés spring up in summer.

DISTANCE 176km (110 miles) one way from Marrakesh; Essaouira tour: 3km (2 miles)

TIME A day (an ideal stay would be 2–3 days)

START Supratours station

END Essaouira beach

POINTS TO NOTE

The easiest and cheapest way to get from Marrakesh to Essaouira is by bus. Supratours runs four coach services daily from the Supratours station (tel: 0524-47 53 17) on Avenue Hassan II, next to the railway station, in Guéliz. Tickets cost 75DH one way and should be booked at least three days in advance, especially at weekends. You will need to book your return journey in Essaouira, again in advance. Bookings can be made by phone, but you must pay in cash on collection. Alternatively, travel by *grand taxi*: a place in a shared taxi will cost about 100DH, or you can charter your own vehicle for around 800DH one way.

An advantage of a hire car is the opportunity to explore the coastline north and south of Essaouira; a disadvantage is that cars are not permitted inside Essaouira's medina, so you will need to find and pay for parking outside the walls; porters with handcarts will transport baggage to wherever you want.

Essaouira has a limited number of sights, but its battlements, fish restaurants, arty vibe and bay should be savoured not rushed, and it is most lovely at night, when day-trippers have returned to Agadir and Marrakesh.

LEAVING MARRAKESH

The journey from Marrakesh takes 2½ hours by coach or *grand taxi (see left)*, including a 20-minute rest stop, or about two hours by hire car. Leave town via Avenue Hassan II, which feeds into the busy N8. This crosses the Haouz Plain, offering distant views of the Atlas on clear days, but otherwise little more than a string of modern settlements and dusty fields.

As you draw near to Essaouira you may see argan trees growing near the roadside. Source of a valuable oil *(see p.95)*, these scrubby, thorny trees, reputed to grow in only two places on Earth – southwest Morocco and Mexico – are magnets for foraging goats.

Food and Drink 🍴

① CAFÉ DRISS
23 Rue Hajjali; tel: 0524-47 57 93; 8am–10pm; $
The best spot for coffee and croissants in town, but also does tasty light meals later in the day.

ON ARRIVAL

Essaouira has expanded far beyond its neat whitewashed medina, but most development stretches north of the town, leaving the old fortified harbour, still the hub of a thriving fishing industry, intact at the head of a magnificent 5km (3 mile) beach. Most accommodation is in riad-style hotels in the medina *(see p.1164)*, including Villa Maroc, a forerunner of the riad phenomenon, and the luxurious l'Heure Bleu; some modern establishments – among them a prominent Sofitel – are starting to encroach along the bay.

From the **Supratours station ❶** (off Avenue Lalla Aicha) head towards the sea, turn right on to Boulevard Mohammed V and follow the road round. It is a few minutes' walk to café-lined **Place Moulay Hassan ❷**, between the harbour and medina and an obvious place to stop for a coffee or cold drink. If you arrive at the main bus station, you could take a *petit taxi* for the 400m/yds or so into town, which will cost around 10DH.

For a light breakfast, head for the back of the square and turn right: the aroma of fresh coffee and baking comes from **Café Driss**, see ⑪①.

Above from far left: Essaouira viewed from the harbour; colourful fishing boats.

Sixties Icons
Essaouira's timeless qualities have attracted artists and musicians, including the Rolling Stones and Jimi Hendrix, since the 1960s.

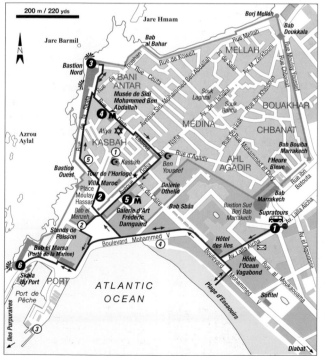

Below: mending nets on the beach; local gulls.

THE MEDINA

In front of Place Moulay Hassan, the esplanade leads down to the harbour, while, behind it, Essaouira's medina spreads inland in a grid pattern. It was laid out in the 18th century by Cornut of Avignon, a Frenchman, and Ahmed el Inglesi, an English captive of Sultan Mohammed ibn Abdullah. Known at that time as Mogador, the town was founded as a free port for European merchants trading in gold, ivory and slaves. The unoccupied Iles Purpuraires, just offshore, provided sheltered anchorage along an otherwise exposed stretch of African coastline; indeed, many centuries previously, the site, then known as Karikon Telichos, had been a trading post for Phoenician traders.

Its European architects gave Mogador straighter streets than is usual in a Moroccan medina, plus a clocktower *(tour de l'horloge)* in Avenue Oqba ibn Nafia and the town's impressive fortifications. Punctuated by towers, turrets and buttresses, these were inspired by St Malo in France. A fine example of an 18th-century fortified seaport translated to a North African setting, Essaouira is a Unesco World Heritage Site.

SHOPPING

Early evening is the best time to shop, but mornings are busy too, with most activity on or off its two main arteries, **Avenue de l'Istiqlal** and **Avenue Sidi Mohammed Ben Abdallah**, which run parallel to one another. Both lead into the old *mellah* or Jewish Quarter *(see box, right)* and eventually to the city gate,

Below: fish for lunch.

Bab Doukkala, beyond of which are the Christian and Jewish cemeteries.

THE SIGHTS

From Place Moulay Hassan take the first left (just past a bank) on to Rue de la Skala and follow round the tall blank walls of the cannon-bristled battlements. Head to the **North Bastion** ❸ (Bastion Nord), where a cluster of carpentry stalls offer hassle-free browsing and the opportunity to see woodworkers at their craft. The richly grained thuya wood of the area is turned into tables, boxes, chessboards, backgammon sets and bowls, often inlaid with pale lemon wood or mother-of-pearl and worked up to a lustrous sheen.

The Ramparts

From here steps lead up on to the **ramparts**. This sweeping scene was chosen for the opening shot in Orson Welles's *Othello* (1952). Welles, who financed the film and played the leading role, spent many months filming in the town, staying all the while in the Hôtel des Iles, which is still going strong on Boulevard Mohammed V. Constrained by tight budgets, he filmed many of the most atmospheric shots in a local hammam.

Museums and Galleries

From the ramparts return to Rue de la Skala and head along Rue Derb Laâlouj, which will take you past the **Sidi Mohammed Ben Abdallah Museum** ❹ (Wed–Mon 9am–6pm; charge), a good place to find out about the town's Jewish and musical heritage as well as its arts and crafts.

Follow the road all the way to Avenue Oqba ibn Nafia and turn right along the avenue. This will take you past one of the better art galleries, **Frédéric Damgaard** ❺ (9am–1pm and 3–7pm), which has been in business for more than 30 years. Also located nearby is **Espace Othello** (9 Rue Mohammed Layachi; 10am–1pm and 3–7pm).

Fish Stands

Follow the avenue to its end to emerge into the area in front of Place Moulay Hassan, where a row of **fish stands**, see ⑪②, do a busy lunchtime trade.

Above from far left: the battlement-enclosed medina; in the woodworking souk; cannons still point through the battlements; Taros, a popular rooftop café *(see p.70)*.

Below: a Jewish baker in the *mellah*.

Essaouira's Jewish Legacy

For a small town, Essaouira has a substantial *mellah* (old Jewish quarter) and Jewish Cemetery (outside Bab Doukkala), reflecting the town's once-significant Jewish population.

Jews were often middlemen for European and Arab merchants; in 1860, the British traveller and writer James Richards estimated that they comprised nearly one third of the town's 13–14,000-strong population. Among the prominent Jewish familes were the Disraelis, whose descendant Benjamin became one of Britain's most distinguished prime ministers. Very few Jews remain today, the majority having emigrated to Israel or Europe in the second half of the 20th century. A tiny synagogue still stands on Rue Ziry Ben Atiyah (off Rue Derb Laâlouj), but it is dilapidated and disused.

Quad Biking

Expect to pay around 300DH an hour to go quad biking in Essaouira. There is usually a lower age limit of 12, and hotel transfer is provided. Palma Quad (70 Boulevard Moham-med V; tel: 066-70 99 99; www.palmaquad. com) offers taster sessions of one and two hours, as well as half- and full-day safaris to Sidi Kaouki.

THE HARBOUR

After lunch walk towards the harbour. To the right is the **Skala du Port** ❻ (8.30am–noon and 2.30–6pm; charge) with more good views, nooks, crannies and cannons – some of British manufacture – to sit on.

At the far end of the harbour, the decrepit-looking **Chez Sam**, see ⑪③, is a long-venerated fish restaurant that comes alive in the evenings.

The harbour offers plenty of nautical activity, with fishing boats large and small unloading their catches at all times of the day.

Boat Trips

Close by, **Promenade en Mer** operates boat trips around the bay at regular intervals and at pretty reasonable cost, allowing passengers a closer look at the **Iles Purpuraires**, just offshore.

In ancient times these islands, like many other such places around the Mediterranean, were a base for the manufacture of a purple dye known as Tyrian purple. The dye, derived from

---

Food and Drink 🍴

③ CHEZ SAM

The Harbour; tel: 0524-47 62 38; noon–3pm and 7–11pm; $$
In spite of new competition aplenty, this long-established ramshackle restaurant with its 'decks', harbour views and great-value lobster menu remains one of the best places in town to eat fish. To find it, walk along the left-hand leg of the fishing harbour, passing the Gendarmerie (police station).

④ CHALET DE LA PLAGE

Avenue Mohammed V; tel: 0524-47 59 72; www.lechaletdela plage.com; noon–1.30pm and 7.30pm–1am; $$
This restaurant *(pictured)*, overlooking the beach at the medina end of Avenue Mohammed V, has been in business since 1893 – before the French Protectorate – and it has bags of character to prove it. If the weather is warm, try to get a table on the seaside terrace at the back; it's a great place to watch the sun set and the waves break upon the shore. The menu features plenty of fish, but it offers good steaks and classic French fare too. You can also just have tapas and a drink at the bar.

⑤ TAROS

Place Moulay Hassan; tel: 0524-47 64 07; www.taroscafe.com; 8am–11pm; closed Sun; $$–$$$
Prominent rooftop café-bar with a mellow buzz that attracts a mixed crowd for daytime lounging and reading and night-time cocktails, supper and live music. Also has a cosy candlelit restaurant, a library and an art gallery. The menu ranges from oysters and lobster to roast duck and good tajines.

the murex shellfish, was very much in demand in 1st-century Rome to create the distinctive stripe on the senators' togas.

During Essaouira's heyday as a port, the islands were used as a quarantine station for pilgrims returning from Mecca, and later, in the 19th century, as a prison, the abandoned buildings of which are still visible on the skyline.

Today the islands have been turned into a bird sanctuary, especially for the Eleanora's falcon, and landings are prohibited.

into the waves is often cited as the inspiration of Jimi Hendrix's *Castles Made of Sand* – although the song was written two years before his visit in 1969.

The far reaches of the beach are also the place to find horse and camel rides, and quad bikes *(see margin, left)*, all available on the spot. For longer rides, with hard hats etc, it is best to book with one of the companies operating out of Diabet (for these and water sport companies, *see pp.22–3*); they will pick you up from your hotel in Essaouira at an agreed time.

Above from far left:
the harbour; football on the beach; the fishing boats attract a hungry visitor; the day's catch.

THE BEACH

Late afternoon is a good time for a walk around the bay, so take a leisurely stroll along Boulevard Mohammed V, or, if you prefer, relax on the beach, where this route ends. On summer evenings the beach is floodlit, allowing football, volleyball and even swimming to continue late into the night.

Options for Dinner
The seaside terrace of **Chalet de la Plage**, see ⑪④, is a good spot to watch the action over a seafood supper and a bottle of *gris*. Among the medina's restaurants and cafés it is hard to beat the rooftop of **Taros**, see ⑪⑤. With its live music, tapas, cocktails and cushions, it is the very definition of chilled.

Diabet and Beach Activities
The main beach stretches for miles, and if you have time, you may wish to walk to the dunes of **Diabet**, taking about 40 minutes. Here, a watchtower sinking

Gnaoua Music Festival

Essaouira's Gnaoua Festival (www.festival-gnaoua.net), which takes place over a long weekend in late June, is one of the highlights in world music's calendar of festivals. Inaugurated in 1998, it now attracts more than 200,000 people, mainly Moroccans, but also an increasing number of foreigners, as knowledge of the event spreads. Rooted in the music of the *Gnaoua*, a black African sect descended from slaves introduced to Morocco in the 11th century, it includes elements of West African and Sufi trance music and also mixes in jazz and blues. Events, which are free, take place in Place Moulay Hassan, Bab Marrakech and on the beach. If you do manage to attend, expect a fairly unorthodox experience, with some members of the audience entering into trancelike states.

THE OURIKA VALLEY

When Marrakesh gets too hot or hectic, locals and visitors alike head for the foothills of the High Atlas. The Ourika Valley is one of the nearest and most accessible of the various destinations on offer outside the city.

DISTANCE 126km (78 miles) round trip

TIME A full day

START/END Marrakesh

POINTS TO NOTE

Despite the poor surface in the Ourika Valley, a non-4x4 vehicle is fine for this tour. The route is relatively easy but many local operators run day trips into the valley. Hiring a private taxi for the day costs around 1,400DH. A *grand taxi* will cost 400DH one way, and take up to six people.

When to Go

The Ourika Valley can be visited at any time of year. In winter the valley is cold and crisp, but rarely snow-covered, and in summer temperatures can be up to 15°C (22.5°F) cooler than in Marrakesh.

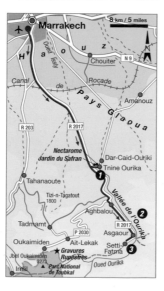

Gazing southward on a clear day from any rooftop in Marrakesh, one cannot but be captivated by the horseshoe of towering mountains that rise up from the flat plain that surrounds the city. Arguably, any visit to the Red City should be complemented by a foray into this impressive range, which is largely responsible for Marrakesh's high proportion of Berbers, a race of mountain dwellers who account for around half of the city's inhabitants.

The Ourika Valley, with its sheltered olive and walnut groves, where water flows year-round, offers a rewarding and convenient day trip into the Atlas, possible by hire car or by private taxi. But be warned that the valley is no longer a well-kept secret, and in summer *Marrakshis* head for the cool waters of the Ourika in their droves.

LEAVING MARRAKESH

Starting at the roundabout just the other side of the city wall from the landmark La Mamounia Hotel *(see p.62)*, follow Boulevard El Yarmouk southward, keeping the ramparts on your left. In winter, and on clear days at other times of year, the panorama of the Atlas Mountains in front of you will confirm that you are heading in the right direction.

Above from far left:
the Ourika Valley; the
Monday market in
Tnine Ourika.

As you leave the city you'll see a familiar picture-postcard shot of the 11th-century ramparts framed by date palms and the mountains. The route cuts across the flat and rather featureless Haouz Plain, on which wealthy Moroccans and foreigners have built lavish villas amid a landscape of olive groves and fruit orchards. Such prosperity has also spawned interior-decoration shops, informal garden centres and artisan workshops, catering to the surge in demand that villas and *maisons d'hôte* in the region have created.

TNINE OURIKA

Follow the road for 33km (20 miles) until you arrive at the first major settlement and continue straight at the roundabout. Keep on for another 500m/yds until you reach a left turn (signposted 'Jardin Nectarome') towards the village of **Tnine Ourika** ❶, a bustling regional centre set in olive groves below the foothills of the Atlas. Tnine means Monday in Arabic, and the town hosts a Monday market that is well worth a visit. Such souks have a hugely important socio-economic role to play in Berber society, but you are unlikely to find any really interesting bargains.

Saffron Garden

Before arriving at the village itself (a few hundred metres after the left turn) a sign will direct you to the **Saffron Garden** (Jardin du Safran; www.safran-ourika.com; daily 9am–6pm; charge). This privately owned saffron garden holds a small museum that demonstrates the various stages in the production of saffron, and all produce

Left: cooking a tajine in Tnine Ourika.

Above from left: pottery workshop; Berber woman; crossing a valley rope-bridge; the turn to Oukaimiden.

Oukaimiden Skiing

The season is short, facilities are rudimentary and there are only a couple of slopes, but the low-key informality of Oukaimiden is part of the charm. You can hire equipment and arrange lessons with the enterprising locals, and there are a couple of hotels: Chez Ju-Ju (tel: 0524-31 90 05; www.hotelchezjuju. com) is a characterful inn. Although it can get busy at weekends, when wealthy *Marrakshis* converge, on weekdays the resort is virtually empty.

Below: the organic Nectarome garden.

is sold on-site to visitors. If you are in Ourika during October or November, a visit to the garden is particularly worthwhile as, at this time of the year, women from the surrounding villages harvest the crop, which takes a year from planting to come to fruition.

Nectarome Garden

Continuing into the village of Tnine, keep your eyes peeled for a sign off to the left to **Nectarome** (daily 9am–6pm; www.nectarome.com; charge), which is accessed by an 800m/yd dirt road (passable in a conventional vehicle) that starts opposite the police station *(Gendarmerie)*, just before the marketplace. This garden is a far more elaborate affair than the saffron garden and bills itself as an 'organic aromatic garden' dedicated to the study of essential oils and natural cosmetics. It is an interesting place to visit and has a shop (as well as an extensive online catalogue) selling the well-being products that are generated on site.

THE OURIKA VALLEY

Retracing your path back to the main road from Marrakesh, turn left at the junction and continue southward. After a few kilometres, the Ourika River comes into view, cutting its way through fairly extensive olive-tree plantations that characterise the **Ourika Valley ❷** (Vallée de l'Ourika). The adobe villages on the far side of the river may be your first taste of rural Morocco, and you will notice that the traditional architecture of these Berber houses has been somewhat eroded on the tarmac-road side of the river. In Morocco, where there's tarmac (and tourism), there's money, and a crop of concrete dwellings (some fairly elaborate) has sprung up along the main road here.

You will also notice that the tourist industry appears to be alive and well in this particular Atlas valley, as bazaars selling carpets and pottery line the route. However, carpets are not native to this region; rather, Ourika is a valley

Food and Drink 🍴

There is an abundance of restaurants lining the Ourika Valley road, and all specialise in Berber home cooking. This plays on the strengths of ingredients available in the immediate vicinity, with lamb or beef stews (tajines) made with locally grown (mainly root) vegetables the preferred main dish, and couscous on Fridays. Corn soups (dshisha), chickpea soup (harira) and bean stews (lubia) are also a popular way to ward off the winter chill of the mountains.

أوكـايمـدن

OUKAIMIDEN

of potteries, and most of the shops have workshops and kilns that you can visit if you are interested. If you do pay a visit you'll be expected to make a small purchase.

If you need some lunch while driving along the valley road there are plenty of Berber restaurants at which to stop *(see the Food and Drink ⑪ box, below left)*.

Mountain Activities

Continuing on from the villages of the lower Ourika, the road winds its way gradually up the increasingly steep-sided valley. At the 43km (26-mile) mark you'll pass a right turn to **Oukaimiden**, which, at 2,700m (8,858ft) above sea level, is North Africa's highest ski station *(see margin, left)*. From the junction the road climbs steeply for around 30km (20 miles) up to the resort, which boasts basic accommodation, two ski lifts and equipment-hire shops. The ski season runs from December to February, but snow can never be guaranteed, even in winter. During the summer months the area offers plenty of interesting and scenic hiking possibilities.

Along the Ourika Road

A few hundred metres after the Oukaimiden turn-off, the village of **Aghbalou** has a small Thursday souk (signposted down a steep track off to the left). Onward from here there are a number of busy villages offering riverside eating facilities popular with Moroccan day-trippers. It is not until the approach to Setti Fatma, though, that the full drama of the High Atlas begins to unfold.

Berber Architecture

The villages that flank the eastern side of the Ourika Valley, and many of the small settlements that line the route up to Oukaimiden, contain excellent examples of Berber High Atlas vernacular, which, in this region, dates back centuries. The architecture is simple and at times austere; few changes have been made to building materials or practices over the years.

Here, construction is all about making use of raw materials that are found in the region, where earth, straw, sand and stone are blended to build dwellings that are both environmentally sound and sit in harmony with their surroundings. Some villagers choose to build their houses with adobe bricks, a strong and resilient mud brick made with a wooden framework and left to dry prior to being laid; others favour *pisé*, a similar mix of earth, straw and sand compressed in between rows of wooden shuttering and left to dry. Roofs are rarely pitched, and are constructed of eucalyptus beams on to which plastic sheeting (for waterproofing) is laid, before a final coat of mud is applied.

The thermal properties of earth houses in the extreme climate of Morocco are unrivalled by most modern building materials, but, as the population grows in wealth, it is expected that traditional building methods will be used less.

Above from left:
lunch by the river at
Setti Fatma; the
Kasbah du Toubkal.

Day Walks

Arrange your hike
through the Bureau
des Guides (tel:
0524-48 56 26) in
Imlil, the centre for
registered guides
in the region. Most
speak English and
you can do treks of
various lengths.

Below: one of the
seven waterfalls
around Setti Fatma.

SETTI FATMA

Setti Fatma ❸, a small but lively trail-head village, is the end of the line for non-4x4 vehicles. Located at the end of the tarmac road, 60km (37 miles) from Marrakesh, the village is hemmed in by towering limestone cliffs.

Hiking Options

Setti Fatma is the staging post for some exciting treks into the heart of the High Atlas. A two-day hike takes you to Oukaimiden *(see p.75)*, and three days of trekking takes you to Imlil *(see p.79)* at the foot of Mount Toubkal, the highest mountain in North Africa.

On arrival in Setti Fatma you may be accosted by locals wishing to take you to the waterfalls above the village or to local bazaars. Choosing an official guide from the Bureau des Guides *(see margin, left)* is a good way to buy some peace and quiet.

For the hikes in the Atlas or up to the waterfalls you will need solid walking shoes suitable for mountainous and rocky terrain. For those seeking a more gentle stroll, continue through the village and follow the river through a U-shaped valley lined with village houses. The scenery here is fabulous.

Of all the many places to eat in the village – most of them serving traditional local food – one of the best is **La Perle d'Ourika** *(see the Food and Drink ❶ box, below)*.

RETURN TO MARRAKESH

After time to enjoy your surroundings, retrace your path back to Marrakesh for an early evening aperitif in your hotel. The journey back, without stops to refuel or shop, takes about an hour and a half.

Food and Drink 🍴

Setti Fatma is teeming with restaurants serving Berber specialities. Try **La Perle d'Ourika** (tel: 061-567239), run by the lovely Ammaria. Otherwise there is a cluster alongside the river. As a rule, opt for the busier restaurants (they will have a faster turnover of food), particularly those that seem popular with locals, or check at the Bureau des Guides which of the many restaurants is currently in favour.

IMLIL AND MOUNT TOUBKAL

Mountain lovers and hikers should head for Imlil, a Berber village in the heart of the Toubkal National Park, amid shady walnut groves at the foot of North Africa's highest peak. The area offers unspoilt scenery, hikes to suit all levels and great accommodation.

Less developed and more authentic than the neighbouring Ourika Valley, the Mizane Valley links the Berber settlements of Asni and Imlil, and offers an enthralling glimpse of life in the High Atlas Mountains. It is a land where mysterious cloaked figures shuffle into mountainside mosques, womenfolk quietly harvest crops in immaculately terraced fields, and the pace of life slows to a virtual standstill.

At the head of the valley, the popular trailhead village of Imlil generates an atmosphere all of its own and makes an excellent base or starting point for walks into the surrounding mountains. A rewarding two-day hike takes you up to the summit of the country's highest peak, but for those not prepared to expend quite so much energy, the area offers some other interesting possibilities, most notably walks in the untouched Tacheddirt Valley, over the Tamatert Pass from Imlil.

LEAVING MARRAKESH

Setting off from the roundabout alongside the city wall at La Mamounia Hotel, head south, keeping the ramparts on your left. Ignore the first right turn (signposted 'aéroport') and take the second right turn a couple of hundred metres further on. This is the R203 (signposted 'Taroudant'), a road

---

DISTANCE 190km (118 miles) round trip

TIME Possible as a long day trip, but better with a night in Imlil

START/END Marrakesh

POINTS TO NOTE

This excursion can be undertaken in a non-4x4 rental vehicle, and all of the route is along tarmac roads. Without a hire car the trip can be undertaken in a private taxi, 4WD will cost around 1,400DH for the day. A *grand taxi* will cost 400DH one way, and take up to six people.

Should you wish to go hiking in Toubkal National Park, the Bureau des Guides in Imlil (*see p.80*) can organise multi-day, fully catered, mule-supported treks. These are best booked at least a few days in advance.

The best time of year to hike in the region is between April and November, when high passes are not blocked by heavy snowfalls.

Booking Ahead

If you are intending to stay the night in the Toubkal National Park, you are advised to reserve your accommodation in advance, particularly during the spring and autumn, when the Imlil area can get extremely busy.

If you plan to do the two-day hike to the summit of Mount Toubkal (*see p.81*), you will need to bring your own sleeping bag to use at the refuge, or a tent.

that eventually runs into the infamous Tizi-n-Test *(see p.95)*, one of the highest and most precipitous passes in North Africa. Along this road be careful to keep your speed below 60kph (37mph) as it is a well-known police speed-trap, and continue until you reach a fork in the road after a further 5km (3 miles) or so. Take the left fork and remain on this rather nondescript route until you arrive in the village of **Tahanaoute**, an important regional centre set in an immense olive grove. Continue straight on at the mini roundabout and follow the road, which, after a few kilometres, begins to climb into the foothills of the High Atlas.

ASNI

The first village you arrive at, some 47km (29 miles) from Marrakesh, is **Asni ❶** *(see also p.93)*, which has an important Saturday souk. The market attracts villagers from far and wide: they descend upon the village every week to trade goods, do business and discuss the week's events over a glass of impossibly sweet mint tea. There's little to see or do in Asni, but it makes a convenient place to stop for a tea or

coffee break en route. Be warned that, on market day, the busy atmosphere might feel overwhelming.

MARIGHA

Just beyond Asni, a left turn (sign-posted 'Imlil') takes you up the Mizane Valley along a scenic route to Imlil and the gateway to the Toubkal National Park. Note this turn-off but continue along the same (Tizi-n-Test) route that snakes its way down a valley of green oak and juniper bushes to the village of **Marigha**, after a further 10km (6 miles).

In the village, which appears from the road to be little more than a few houses, turn right at the crossroads (signposted 'Amizmiz') and then turn right into the car park of **L'Oliveraie de Marigha**, see ⑪①, where you can have some lunch and relax by the pool.

MIZANE VALLEY

After lunch head back up the winding road towards Asni and take the Imlil turn-off (on your right). The 17km (10-mile) road passes through the **Mizane Valley** (Vallée de Mizane), where a thin strip of cultivation on the valley floor is framed by stark peaks, and traditional mud villages cling to the hillsides. The Mizane river flows year-round and irrigates villagers' vegetable patches and groves of walnut and almond trees.

Kasbah Tamadot

After a few kilometres you will pass **Kasbah Tamadot** *(see p.115)*, Richard

Accommodation Options

The Marigha/Ouirgane area boasts several good places to stay, including the Provençal-style La Bergerie *(see p.114)*, the elegant Domaine de la Roseraie *(see 5)* and the traditional Berber lodge Dar Tassa *(pictured;* tel: 0524-48 43 12).

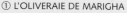

Food and Drink ⑪

① L'OLIVERAIE DE MARIGHA
Marigha, Route d'Amizmiz par Asni; tel: 0524-48 42 81; www.oliveraie-de-marigha.com; 10am–11pm; $–$$
Set in olive groves and affording excellent views of the surrounding foothills, this Provençal-style garden restaurant serves light lunches such as salads and brochettes (skewers) and offers diners use of its excellent swimming pool (non-diners 150DH). Alcohol served.

Branson's hotel retreat, a rambling kasbah-style building set in lavish gardens overlooking the valley. It's luxurious, with prices to match.

IMLIL

Arriving in **Imlil** ➋, look out for a sign welcoming you to the **Toubkal National Park** (Parc National du Toubkal), one of the main reasons for visiting this bustling High Atlas village. Continue into the village, where you'll see a parking area to the left after a couple of hundred metres (next to the Bureau des Guides). Here you can leave your car with the parking attendant for 5DH.

Imlil is arguably the High Atlas's most commercial village, but is surrounded by extraordinary scenery. Here, Moroccan day-trippers congregate along the river banks and hikers start and finish the trek up Mount Toubkal, the highest mountain in Africa to the north of the equator.

Kasbah du Toubkal

In the village walk up the main street (left out of the car park), then take the first right (after a couple of

Above from far left: the Mizane Valley (Kasbah Tamadot is located within the clump of trees to the right); the main street in Imlil.

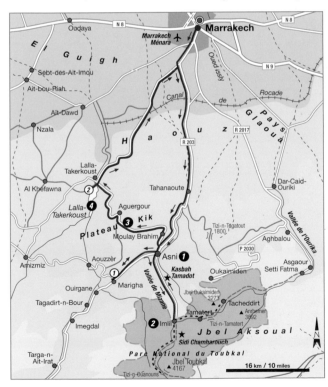

hundred metres), along a road lined with souvenir shops. From here follow signs along a steep (and moderately strenuous) winding track shaded by walnut trees up to the **Kasbah du Toubkal** (tel: 0524-48 56 11), a British-owned hotel with a wonderful location overlooking the valley. The hotel, which doubled as a Tibetan temple in the Scorsese film *Kundun*, has rooms ranging from basic dormitories to luxurious suites, and has a unique location, impressive eco-lodge credentials and offers opportunities for mule-trekking in the surrounding countryside. If you want to stay at this hotel it is essen-

tial to book in advance. The 15- to 20-minute walk up to the site is worth the effort, whether you go inside the Kasbah or not.

Guide Services

Returning to Imlil, head back to the car park and visit the **Bureau des Guides** (tel: 0524-48 56 26) on the left as you face the river. Here you can find maps of the area, plus assistance and advice regarding trekking in the region. Local guides (and mules to carry bags) are usually available at short notice. For those wanting to tackle the summit of Toubkal, now is your chance to make an arrangement – if you have

not done so in advance with a tour company – to start the two- to three-day walk the next day.

Climbing Toubkal

From Imlil it takes two days to reach the summit of **Mount Toubkal**, (Jbel Toubkal), which, at 4,167m (13,671ft) above sea level, is North Africa's highest mountain. The well-trodden path south from Imlil, at 1,500m (5,000ft), up to the roof of North Africa, is a remorseless hike, broken by an overnight stop at the CAF (Club Alpin Français) refuge at some 3,200m (10,500ft).

The first day's walk is a five- to six-hour haul up from Imlil, via the holy shrine *(marabout)* of **Sidi Chamha-rouch**, to the well-equipped, but rather bleak, **CAF refuge**. Here you can turn up and be served a hot meal and sleep in a dormitory with other trekkers (you'll need to bring your own sleeping bag), and there is also a rocky camping area downstream from the refuge for those equipped with tents.

The ascent follows a path leading eastwards from the refuge and includes some steep sections towards the top of the climb. While the hike doesn't involve any rock climbing, it should be considered strenuous and steep enough to deter those who are not accustomed to mountain trekking. To tackle the climb, try to set off early, as clouds often close in on the summit after midday. The walk up from the refuge takes about three hours; fit walkers can then return to Imlil on the same day, rather than stay another night in the uninspiring refuge. On a clear day the views from the top of Toubkal, out towards the northern fringes of the Sahara Desert, are magnificent, making the peak a worthy challenge.

Tamatert Pass and Tacheddirt

Those wanting to stay overnight in the Imlil area are recommended to stay at **Douar Samra** (tel: 0524 37 86 05; www.douar-samra.com), a stylish Berber guesthouse in the hamlet of **Tamatert**, 3km (2 miles) east of Imlil. This sublime adobe house, owned by the enigmatic Jacqueline Brandt, is perched high above Imlil and offers both amazing views and excellent Moroccan home-cooking. Rooms should be booked in advance, at which point you'll be given instructions on how to find the place, which is lost in a maze of mud houses and walnut trees.

Note that the road to Douar Samra from Imlil is unpaved, but the road is passable in a conventional car, except after heavy rain.

Douar Samra is situated approximately halfway up the **Tamatert Pass**, over which lies the village of **Tacheddirt**, said to be the highest village of its size in the High Atlas. Set in a wide rolling valley, Tacheddirt and its neighbouring villages are a delight, and the valley makes for some interesting and rewarding walking. Day hikes with an English-speaking guide can be arranged from Douar Samra up the pass; these will take you through some glorious villages that are still isolated enough to preserve a fiercely traditional way of life.

Be Prepared
The Toubkal National Park is subject to rapid changes in climatic conditions, so make sure that you pack appropriate clothing. Waterproof and windproof jackets are essential (even in summer), as are stout, well-worn-in hiking boots for trekking along the area's rocky trails.

Winter Ascents
The upper slopes of Toubkal are usually snow-covered from late November to June, so during this period the summit is recommended only for those with snow-climbing experience. Though crampons can be hired in Imlil, the quality of the equipment on offer is often substandard, so you're better off bringing your own. Although certified mountain guides (ask to see their official ID cards) have received training in snow climbing, you are recommended to book winter ascents through a bona-fide tour operator.

Above from left: a town on the Kik Plateau; paragliding over the plateau; a keeper of a kasbah; the Draa Valley.

New Horizons
The piste that leads from Imlil to Tacheddirt has now been surfaced, connecting Imlil with Oukaimiden (see p.74), the ski resort that lies over a precipitous pass from Tacheddirt. This has opened up the region even more to visitors, and the village now has electricity, so things are changing fast.

Alfresco Lunch
In spring, an appealing option is to take a picnic on to the Kik Plateau. Most hotels will prepare a picnic for you, if you ask the night before your departure. The views down towards Lalla-Takerkoust and the town of Amizmiz are quite breathtaking.

Right: the lake of Lalla-Takerkoust.

OVER THE KIK PLATEAU

After a night or two in the mountains, head back on the road to Asni. Turn left at the T-junction and then drive through Asni on the road towards Tahanaoute and Marrakesh. Shortly after the avenue of eucalyptus trees at the exit to the village you will come to a left turn. Continue along this tarmac road up to **Moulay Brahim**, a rather untidy mountain-top village that attracts a mixed crowd of pilgrims and day-trippers from Marrakesh. There is really nothing here to interest foreign visitors, so pass quickly through the village.

Continue to the **Kik Plateau** ❸, a rolling expanse of wheat fields (in season) punctuated by scenic hamlets and overlooked by some of the highest peaks in the Atlas range.

The plateau loses some of its appeal in the dry summer and early autumn months, but during late winter and throughout spring, when fields of poppies are framed by dramatic snow-capped mountains, it is one of the most magical places in the High Atlas. You can take a walk here, or, if you are driving a 4x4 vehicle, you can venture off-road on one of the pistes that traverse the area.

THE LAKE OF LALLA-TAKERKOUST

Follow the newly laid tarmac road across the plateau and then down on to the Haouz Plain, where you will find the lake of **Lalla-Takerkoust** ❹. This barrage is the source of most of Marrakesh's water, which is carried down to the city along man-made canals.

The lake is a pleasant enough spot for a stroll, and the French-owned hotel/restaurant **Relais du Lac**, see ⑪②, on the far shore, is a good bet for lunch.

RETURN TO MARRAKESH

From the restaurant head back around the lake and turn right on to the main road, from where it is a 33km (20-mile) drive back to Marrakesh.

Food and Drink

② RELAIS DU LAC
Route du Lac, Route d'Amizmiz, Lalla-Takerkoust; tel: 0524-48 49 43; daily, all day; $$
This pleasant lakeside restaurant has superb views over the Lalla-Takerkoust Lake and out to the High Atlas foothills. It serves simple Moroccan (tajines and couscous) and French (steak and brochettes) cuisine, with indoor and outdoor dining available.

TIZI-N-TICHKA TO ZAGORA

No visit to Morocco would be complete without a foray into the south, a landscape of crumbling kasbahs, oases and wide open spaces. With spectacular scenery and a growing number of excellent guesthouses, the south side of the High Atlas offers adventure and comfort in equal measure.

The sweeping plains and lonely mountain ranges south of Tizi-n-Tichka (Tichka Pass) have some of Morocco's most captivating sights. The Unesco World Heritage Sites of Ait Benhaddou and the Draa Valley are just two highlights of the journey from the High Atlas Mountains to the Sahara Desert. In fact, no other region of Morocco illustrates so beautifully the transition, both in human and physical terms, between mountain and desert. For those with time and a hire car, the journey from Marrakesh to Zagora is highly recommended.

LEAVING MARRAKESH

Starting from the bus station at Bab Doukkala, drive out of the city on the Fez road, heading east with the city wall on your right. This road takes you for a kilometre or so around the perimeter of the medina, until you reach a roundabout with the Bab el Khemis market on your right.

Here, continue straight on for 7km (4 miles), passing the Metro hypermarket (on your right), before turning right at a major roundabout. This is where you join the N9, a road that

DISTANCE 850km (528 miles) round trip

TIME Recommended as a 3- or 4-day trip

START/END Marrakesh

POINTS TO NOTE

This tour can be undertaken in a rental vehicle, and, apart from a short sandy section to the dunes of Tinfou and a rough jeep-road to Oasis Fint, all of the route is surfaced. While bus services exist between Marrakesh and Ouarzazate, and Ouarzazate and Zagora, this tour is hard to accomplish this way as there are many stops en route. Book ahead for hotels and restaurants.

When to Go

The best times to travel around this area are spring and autumn. You are strongly advised to avoid the blistering summer months (July–Sept), when cauldron-like temperatures make this trip impractical (as many tourist services are closed), and extremely uncomfortable.

Left: Kasbah Tamnougalte *(see p.89)* in the Draa Valley.

eventually climbs over the spine of the Atlas Mountains before dropping down to the city of Ouarzazate.

Across the Haouz Plain

As with all routes out of the city, the road traverses the **Haouz Plain**, a relatively fertile and prosperous region where olive groves and citrus orchards dominate the landscape. As you drive across the plain you'll see the occasional villa complex catering to wealthy Moroccans and expats.

THE ATLAS FOOTHILLS

Continuing along this road you'll pass the market town of **Ait-Ourir ❶**, which has an interesting Tuesday souk on the left side of the main road. It's a friendly Berber market that's well worth a visit, though there is nothing else of particular note in the town.

Past the town, which lies 36km (22 miles) from Marrakesh, the topography begins to change as the foothills of the High Atlas start to make an impression on the landscape. After the fertile **Zat Valley** (Vallée du Zat, on your right), olive trees give way to pines, juniper and green oak, as the road climbs into the mountains. If you want a break there are a number of cafés offering panoramic mountain views from their terraces.

Taddert

Carry on to **Taddert ❷**, a bustling pit-stop village at the foot of the winding Tichka Pass. You may not fancy the rows of meat hanging in the roadside butchers' shops (choose your cut and

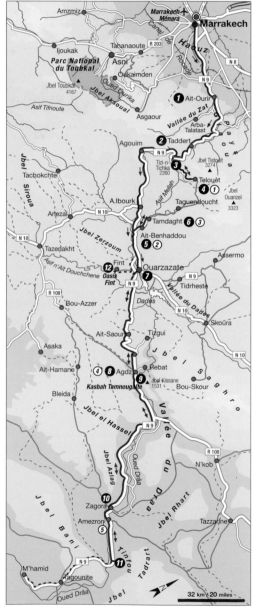

COL DU TICHKA
ALT 2260

then choose a restaurant to barbeque it for you), but it is a good place to buy snacks or stop for refreshments.

TIZI-N-TICHKA

After Taddert, which lies some 99km (61 miles) from Marrakesh, the road snakes its way up a series of breath-taking switchbacks, before a flatter section leads you to the top of the Col du Tichka (Tichka Pass). At 2,260m (7,414ft) above sea level, the pass is one of North Africa's highest paved roads. The top of the **Tizi-n-Tichka ❸** is announced by souvenir shops and a café, where you can expect the hard-sell treatment should you decide to stop.

TELOUET

A few kilometres over the top of the Tichka Pass you'll reach a left turn marked 'Telouèt'. Turn down this poorly surfaced tarmac road and continue for 20km (12 miles) until you come to the village of **Telouèt ❹**, home to one of Morocco's most celebrated **kasbahs** (walled fortresses or walled quarters

of a medina). To reach it, continue through the village and then turn right immediately after an elaborate stone-clad restaurant, the **Auberge Telouèt**, see ①. This takes you into the kasbah complex, where you can park.

The Kasbah

Telouèt was built over four centuries (from the 17th to 20th) but gained particular notoriety as the residence of Thami el Glaoui, a Berber tribal chief, ex-governor of Marrakesh and supporter of the French during the protectorate period. After Morocco was granted independence in 1956, the Glaoui family was left disgraced and dispossessed, and Thami el Glaoui died of natural causes soon after.

Since then, Telouèt has remained uninhabited and these days is a crumbling, elegant ruin, a shadow of its once-spectacular self. For a small fee (10DH or so, payable to the custodian on the door) you can have a look round the most recently built quarter of the kasbah. The older section of the kasbah (to the right as you drive down the access road) can be viewed from the

Above from far left: the view from the Col du Tichka; sign marking the altitude.

Off-Road Adventure
If you've rented a 4x4 vehicle, and you have previous off-road driving experience, then consider taking the spectacular piste from Telouèt to Ait Benhaddou. The route, which follows the scenic Ounila Valley southwards, is a continuation of the tarmac road that passes through Telouet. Be warned, though: the piste is extremely rough.

Food and Drink 🍴
① AUBERGE TELOUET
Entrance to Kasbah Telouèt; tel: 0524-89 07 17; daily lunch and dinner; $

This restaurant is a good option for a set lunch (of tajine or couscous) under a camel-hair tent overlooking the Telouèt kasbah. It is worth noting, though, that it can be crowded with day-trippers and 4x4 parties.

Left: view of Telouèt from the kasbah.

Carpet Scam

On the road immediately south of the Tichka Pass, don't stop for anyone requesting help with a supposedly broken-down vehicle. Fake breakdowns of this nature are a popular scam for getting persistent and unscrupulous locals into tourists' cars to take them to carpet shops.

Below: the *ksar* of Ait Benhaddou.

rooftop, but, as you will see, is little more that a pile of crumbling earth inhabited by a family of storks.

After visiting the kasbah, try the restaurants serving simple tagines, around the central square, for lunch.

INTO THE SOUTH

After lunch, drive back to the Tichka Pass and turn left, continuing on your way towards Ouarzazate. This well-maintained road winds through a number of roadside villages before straightening out as it leaves the mountains. Check the roadside distance markers, as you'll need to turn left 23km (14 miles) before Ouarzazate.

The left turn, about 65km (40 miles) from the point where you rejoined the Tichka Pass, is signposted 'Tamdaght' and 'Ait-Benhaddou' and is relatively easy to spot. Heading north along this road you'll have the whole majestic panorama of the High Atlas in front of you as you drive through a desolate landscape dotted with the occasional date palm. After 9km (5 miles) you'll arrive at a village where you'll see a parking area off to your right. Here you can leave the car and walk down a cobbled alleyway (running the gauntlet of souvenir shops) to the riverbed and the Ait-Benhaddou *ksar* (fortified village).

AIT BENHADDOU

The fortified village of **Ait-Benhaddou** ❺ is as good an example of kasbah architecture as you will get in Morocco. The earliest buildings in the complex, which is still inhabited by a handful of families, date back to the 11th century, and the whole village has been designated a Unesco World Heritage Site. It is also popular with filmmakers, and has starred various Hollywood epics, including *Lawrence of Arabia*, *Jesus of Nazareth* (for which it was carefully reconstructed) and *Alexander*.

Here, you can wander around the warren of streets and alleyways, and some of the locals will be happy to show you around their houses for a small fee (10DH or so). After visiting the site there are numerous cafés, restaurants and *auberges* in the newer part of town, near the car park. A good choice is **Dar Mouna**, see ⓣ②.

TAMDAGHT

Continue north in the same direction for a further 6km (4 miles) along the road from Ait Benhaddou. A spectacular ruined kasbah overlooking a valley of almond trees announces your arrival at Tamdaght ❻, another village on an important trade route that connected Marrakesh with the Draa Valley and the Sahara Desert.

Just before the end of the tarmac road, with the kasbah on your left, is a short section of piste that takes you into the *ksar.* Then follow the signs to **Kasbah Ellouze**, see ⑪③, a stylish guesthouse run by a French couple. This comfortable 10-bedroom *maison d'hôte* comes

as quite a surprise, lost among the crumbling ruins of Morocco's turbulent past, and makes an excellent and uncommercial overnight stay, with good food.

OUARZAZATE

Starting out on day two, head back to the Marrakesh–Ouarzazate road and turn left. After 23km (14 miles), you will reach the town of **Ouarzazate ❼**, a rather nondescript administrative centre that grew up as a base of the French Foreign Legion. The town is something of a crossroads between Marrakesh to the north, the Draa Valley *(see p.88)* to the south, the Dades and Todra gorges to the east

(see p.88)

Above from far left: Ait Benhaddou; Glaoui cannon at the entrance to Kasbah Taourirt in Ouarzazate; Kasbah Ellouze; Kasbah Taourirt.

Below: Russell Crowe and Ridley Scott on the set of *Gladiator.*

Food and Drink 🍴

② DAR MOUNA

Ksar Ait Benhaddou; tel: 028-84 30 54; daily for lunch and dinner; $$
As impressive views go, Dar Mouna's panorama of Ait Benhaddou is hard to beat. This adobe guesthouse serves home-cooked Moroccan cuisine on the terrace, or, in the evening, in the rustic dining room. As this is a hotel, you have to settle for a set menu, but the food is of reliably high quality.

③ KASBAH ELLOUZE

Kasbah Tamdaght, Tamdaght; tel: 0524-89 04 59; www.kasbah ellouze.com; daily, non-guests for dinner only; $$
Run by a French chef, Michel Guillen, Kasbah Ellouze is a stylish converted kasbah guesthouse that serves a set menu of soup/salad, followed by fish or meat tajine and a dessert. Non-guests must reserve in advance.

Local Film Industry

Since Orson Welles' 1952 classic, *Othello,* was filmed in Essaouira, Morocco has attracted foreign film-makers seduced by the country's clear light and amazing landscapes. Focus has now shifted to the kasbahs and deserts of the south: *Lawrence of Arabia* and, more recently, *Gladiator* are just two in a long line of epics filmed around Ouarzazate, the home of Moroccan cinema. Proximity to Europe, an excellent infrastructure, minimal bureaucracy and the availability of cheap labour are further incentives for film companies.

With a host of new projects under way and numerous proposals on the drawing board for future works, the Moroccan film industry continues to go from strength to strength.

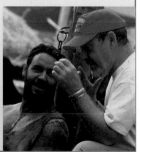

and Taroudant *(see p.96)* and Agadir *(see p.97)* to the west. Notice on your way into town a couple of giant foreign-owned film studios, which further underline the importance of the film industry to the region *(see box, p.87)*.

Kasbah Taourirt

In the town itself, the only attraction of any real note is the **Kasbah Taourirt** (on the main road at the far end of town; no phone; daily 8am–6pm; charge), whose **Glaoui Palace**, part of which is open to the public, has some fine painted wooden ceilings. Much of the rest of the kasbah village is inhabited and is a pleasant place for a stroll.

THE DRAA VALLEY

Starting at the kasbah, drive back into the centre of town, and turn left at a set of traffic lights just before the shops, with the **tourist office** on your left. This route takes you across the river on

what is effectively a continuation of the N9 road from Marrakesh.

Once you have crossed to the south side of the river, bear left, still staying on the same road, and after a couple of kilometres you will leave the urban sprawl of Ouarzazate behind. The road to Agdz (and then eventually Zagora) leads through an undulating moonscape, winding its way up bare volcanic slopes before eventually dropping down into the **Draa Valley** (Vallée du Draa) – a swathe of intensive cultivation in an otherwise barren land.

The Draa river, although dry for much of its course, is the country's longest, and the section of the valley that lies between Ouarzazate and Zagora is home to an estimated eight million date palms *(see margin tip, left)*.

Agdz

The first riverside settlement is **Agdz** ❽, named, some say, after the letters emblazoned on the side of a plane that

Cash Crop
The Draa Valley is a major date-producing region. Only the female date palms bear fruit, with each tree producing about 80kg (176lb) of dates. The date harvest is in November, when locals shin up the trees, cut down the dates and sun-dry them on woven mats.

Right: date palms along the River Draa.

crashed in the valley in the early 1900s. On arrival, pass through the arch and, at the point where the main road dog-legs right, turn left down a side street. Continue for a few hundred metres along this road, keeping a lookout for a right-turn marked 'Dar Qamar'.

Follow the narrow dirt road between two mud walls to a green gate into the guesthouse's car park. **Dar Qamar**, see ⑪④, is a French-owned *maison d'hôte* buried deep in the Agdz kasbah. You can have lunch here (book ahead), and, for those with more time to spare, this magnificent spot with hammam and swimming pool makes an appealing overnight stay *(see p.115)*.

Kasbah Tamnougalte

After lunch, head back to the Ouarza-zate–Zagora road and then turn left towards Zagora. After 5km (3 miles), at a right-hand bend in the road, you will see a piste that crosses one of the channels of the Draa river. Turn left here and follow the unpaved road, which is rough in places but passable, skirting an impressive kasbah perched upon a hill to your left.

Continue until you reach a right turn (after another 500m/yds and easy to miss) and follow this track through an archway into a small parking area. To your right you will see the entrance to **Kasbah Tamnougalte** ❾ (daily 9am–6pm; charge). Here you can pay an English-speaking guide to show you around this well-preserved 16th-century house that was formerly the residence of the *Caïd* (district administrator) of the region. He lived here

with his harem, and the house is now something of a museum piece.

To the left of this kasbah is the guest-house **Chez Yacob** (tel: 0524-84 33 94), itself a restored kasbah that preserves many of its original features, and is also somewhere to have a cup of tea or a meal in the restaurant. After visiting the kasbah drive back to the main road and turn left towards Zagora.

Towards Zagora

From the turn-off point, it is just over 90km (55 miles) to Zagora, along one of the most fascinating routes in Morocco. The villages of the Draa feel intrinsically more African than their counterparts in the High Atlas: a reflection of the fact that the Draa served as a major trade route from sub-Saharan Africa during the 16th and 17th centuries.

As you drive further south you will also start to notice the physical impact of the Sahara Desert on the landscape, as acacia and tamarind trees dominate an increasingly desertified terrain. To the east, the anvil-shaped **Jbel Kissane**

Above from far left: the Dar Qamar guest-house in Agdz; Kasbah Tamnougalte.

Off-Road Options On your way down the Draa Valley, look out for signs (on your left) marked 'Circuit de la Palmeraie'. These access roads allow you into the heart of the Draa's magnificent date-palm plantations. For those with a 4x4 vehicle, note that there is an excellent piste that you can take from Tamnou-galte southwards; it runs parallel to the main road.

> ### Food and Drink 🍴
>
> **④ DAR QAMAR**
> Kasbah d'Agdz, Agdz; tel: 0524-84 37 84; www.locsudmaroc.com; daily for lunch and dinner; $$
> Dar Qamar, an oasis of comfort in the crumbling Agdz kasbah, is a guesthouse that serves meals (lunch or dinner) by advance booking. The food served is generally Moroccan (the obligatory tajine or couscous), and part of a set menu that is included for guests on half-board.

marks the gateway to the magnificent **Jbel Saghro**, a winter trekking paradise accessed from the attractive adobe village of **N'kob**, a turn-off some 29km (18 miles) south of Agdz.

ZAGORA AND TINFOU

As you continue further south, the *palmeraies* (palm groves) become evermore dense, and the town of **Zagora** ⑩, with its breeze-block architecture and frenetic main boulevard, comes as a bit of a shock, even a disappointment, after the journey.

There's not a great deal to see in Zagora, but for sand-dune enthusiasts, daylight hours permitting, you can continue through the town (on the road to Mhamid) towards the dunes of **Tinfou** ⑪, 28km (17 miles) southeast of Zagora.

Tinfou is a cluster of sand dunes on a wide, sweeping plain flanked by the **Jbel Tadrart** mountain range. It is rather a touristy scene at the dunes (signposted left from the main road), so prepare to receive some attention from locals touting camel rides, which are readily available to those who are interested.

Desert Adventure
For a real taste of the desert you'll have to continue a further 96km (60 miles) south from Zagora to the end of the tarmac road. The town of Mhamid offers hotel services and trips into the dunes, staying in permanent tent camps in the shifting sands of the Sahara. For this side-trip you will have to set aside a minimum of an extra two days.

Right: locals offer camel rides at the dunes of Tinfou.

The true dunes of the Sahara begin approximately 70km (43 miles) south in **M'hamid**, at the end of the tarmac road. A trip to M'hamid is beyond the scope of this itinerary, but you might consider extending your trip to incorporate a desert safari starting from there *(see margin tip, left)*.

Accommodation Options

After watching the sunset from the Tinfou dunes, drive back to Zagora and check in to your hotel, which you are advised to have booked in advance. The **Fibule du Draa** (tel: 0524-84 73 18) is an efficient three-star hotel on the southeast side of the river, with a restaurant and an appealing pool, see ⑤, but for a flavour of the Moroccan south try **Dar Raha** (tel: 0524-84 69 93; www.darraha.com) in **Amezrou**, a village situated one kilometre south of Zagora. Run by a French anthropologist, Dar Raha is a sober but stylish adobe house with reasonably priced simple rooms and delicious home-cooking for its guests. The intellectual owner, Antoine

Bouillon, will be delighted to show you round the historic village and explain his work to increase local awareness and knowledge about the patrimony of the Draa.

RETURN VIA OUARZAZATE

The 368km (228-mile) journey back to Marrakesh is possible in a (very long) day, but it is recommended that you break the journey en route in Ouarzazate. Drive back up the Draa Valley, passing through Agdz, and continue towards Ouarzazate.

On the edge of the city, just before you reach the first houses, look for a signpost to the *maison d'hôte* **Dar Daïf** *(see p.115)* and then follow the signs to this attractive and comfortable guest house overlooked by the scenic ruins of the Stork's Kasbah (Kasbah de la Cigogne).

Oasis Fint

Drive back the following morning to the main road and turn left at the first junction (rather than crossing the river to go into the centre of the city). This route is effectively a bypass that rejoins the Ouarzazate–Marrakesh road after a few kilometres. For those who have the time, a left turn off this route (signposted 'Fint') takes you along a rocky unpaved road to one of the most picturesque oases in southern Morocco; a veritable paradise for photographers. After **Oasis Fint** ⑫, return to the main road and then continue back over the Tizi-n-Tichka (Tichka Pass) and down to Marrakesh.

Above from far left: Oasis Fint; sand dunes at Tinfou.

Below: signposts in Zagora.

TIZI-N-TEST
TO TAROUDANT

For a smaller, mellower version of Marrakesh, head over the dramatic pass of Tizi-n-Test to Taroudant, an attractive walled city in the fertile Souss Valley. Along the way are souks, striking rammed-earth ramparts and, perhaps surprisingly, one of Africa's most exclusive hotel hideaways.

Planning the Drive

As with most mountainous routes in Morocco, allow more time than you expect to cover pre-planned distances. For instance, the drive from Ouirgane to the top of the Tizi-n-Test will take you at least two hours to complete. Also, bear in mind that there are no petrol stations between Asni and Olad Berhil. Be aware that visibility can be hampered by low cloud.

> **DISTANCE** 446km (280 miles) returning via Tizi-n-Test; 765km (475 miles) via Agadir
> **TIME** 2–3 days
> **START/END** Marrakesh
> **POINTS TO NOTE**
>
> The Tizi-n-Test from Marrakesh to Taroudant is a paved road, which, although in need of resurfacing in places, is perfectly manageable in a basic hire vehicle. Private and collective taxis also operate along this route, as do public bus services, but really to take advantage of the journey and its associated stops en route you are recommended to hire a car. If you wish to visit the Agoundis Valley, it is necessary to hire a 4x4 vehicle.
>
> Note that the tour ends with an option to return via Agadir on the coast.

Of all the mountain passes in Morocco, Tizi-n-Test is arguably the most dramatic. The pass marks the watershed between the more fertile northern slopes of the High Atlas and the largely barren south, and the dizzying route offers a great variety of landscapes all the way from the Atlas foothills around Asni to the beautiful panoramas that unfold as you reach the southern face of the range.

Taroudant, the city that marks the furthest point of the tour, is an interesting destination and offers a gateway to the magnificent Anti-Atlas Mountains and the beaches of the deep south of Morocco. This tour can be completed in a quick two-day escape from Marrakesh, but to do the whole region justice, it is recommended that you allow more time.

LEAVING MARRAKESH

Starting from the roundabout at La Mamounia Hotel, follow the city wall southwards (with the wall to your left and the Atlas Mountains directly in front of you) and turn right at the second turning you come to, signposted 'Taroudant'.

Food and Drink 🍴

① LA BERGERIE

Marigha, Route du Tizi-n-Test; tel: 0524-48 57 17; www.labergerie-maroc.com; $$–$$$
La Bergerie is a Provençal-style guesthouse that serves a menu of Moroccan and French dishes. The cosy restaurant has an attractive patio with views of the surrounding hills.

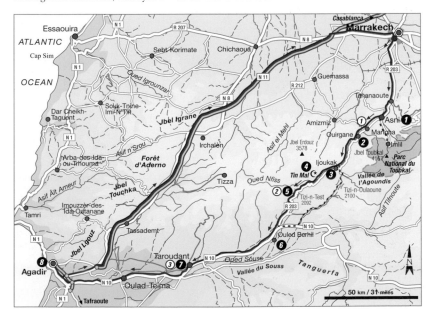

TIZI N'TEST
ALTITUDE DE 2100 M
ROUTE CONSTRUITE PAR LE SERVICE
DES TRAVAUX PUBLICS DU MAROC
1926-1932
MM JOYANT DIRECTEUR GENERAL
DELANDE INGENIEUR EN CHEF
MARTIN INGENIEUR ORDINAIRE
CONTANT INGENIEUR SUBDIVISIONNAIRE
GAUTHIER INGENIEUR ADJOINT

INTO THE HIGH ATLAS

After about 5km (3 miles), follow the road round to the left (ignoring the right-hand fork to Amizmiz) and continue for a further 29km (18 miles) to **Tahanaoute**, a local administrative town and gateway to the foothills of the High Atlas. Pass through the town, staying on the same road, and follow the winding, mountainous route to the Berber village of **Asni ❶** *(see also p.78)*, some 47km (29 miles) from Marrakesh. Asni has a rather intimidating Saturday souk (market), where the locals can get quite pushy, but otherwise it is a reasonable place to stop for a tea break.

Now continue through the village, sticking to the main road, where you'll notice a left turn up to the village of Imlil (covered in more detail in tour 12; *see p.79*), which, for those with time, makes a rewarding side-trip. The 17km (11-mile) road to the village at the foot of North Africa's highest peak is a scenic drive that takes about half an hour in each direction.

Lunch Stop

Back on the Marrakesh–Taroudant road, follow the winding section down to the village of **Marigha** *(see p.78)*, continue through the village and look out for a right-hand turn to **La Bergerie**, see ⓧ①, after a further 500m/ yds. This French-owned *maison d'hôte* makes a good lunch stop, particularly as there are very few other places to eat on the Tizi-n-Test road.

Above from far left: craft shop in a derelict van; dramatic view of the Tizi-n-Test; altitude marker; stall selling fossils such as ammonites.

Ouirgane

After lunch, continue along the Tizi-n-Test, passing through, after a further 3km (2 miles), the village of **Ouirgane** ❷. Sleepy Ouirgane used to be one of the High Atlas's most appealing villages, but the construction of a dam (of the River N'Fis) has had a major impact on the surrounding physical environment and on the lives of the villagers.

Many of the houses in the village have been destroyed, and Ouirgane, for the moment at least, has been transformed into something of a construction site. Water shortages caused by drought and large-scale tourist developments (particularly golf courses) have forced the government to dam even more rivers in the High Atlas in order to cater for the astronomical water demands generated by Marrakesh.

THE N'FIS RIVER VALLEY

Passing through Ouirgane, continue up the Tizi-n-Test. A right-hand bend in the road some 33km (21 miles) from Ouirgane signals your arrival in the village of **Ijoukak** ❸.

Off-Road Options from Ijoukak

To the left, just before the bridge, takes you up the beautiful **Agoundis Valley**, where a thin strip of bright cultivation is flanked by towering limestone rock faces. Note: the piste is fairly rough and can occasionally be impassable without a 4x4 vehicle. Those with suitable transport (and some off-road experience) might also consider the superb 72km (45-mile) route down to the Ouarzazate–Taroudant road (N10). To take this route, continue for another 9km (6 miles), cross the river and then climb sharply up to the **Tizi-n-Oulaoune** pass. Stay on the same route south until you eventually arrive at the main road. The scenery is fabulous, but be aware that this route is very remote, and there are no services.

Tin Mal Mosque

For those continuing on the tarmac route, follow the road through Ijoukak for a further 7km (4½ miles) before arriving at the Tin Mal Mosque, signposted (although not very clearly) to your right. Follow the tarmac road down, over the river and then up to the mosque, where there is an unpaved parking area. You can leave your car with the custodian who will also let you look around the mosque for 10DH.

Tin Mal ❹ was built in 1153 and is one of Morocco's more important historical sites. The 12th-century mosque was the birthplace of the Almohad movement that eventually gave rise to the Berber dynasty of the same name. This mosque, which is roughly contemporary with the Koutoubia *(see p.30)* in Marrakesh, was renovated in the 1990s, having been in an advanced state of decay, and is now one of the few mosques in Morocco that can be visited by non-Muslims. Although it is not currently used by worshippers, there are plans to reopen the mosque in the near future for the collective Friday prayer.

THE TIZI-N-TEST

After the Tin Mal Mosque the road narrows and eventually winds its way up to the top of the **Tizi-n-Test ❺** at 2,092m (6,799ft) above sea-level. En route, a few kilometres/miles before the pass, a piste off to the right leads into the heart of the Western High Atlas, a remote and seldom-visited region that is home to the beautiful **Tichka Plateau**.

A four- or five-day trek takes you to the plateau, and down into the villages on the southern side of the watershed, finishing some way north of the town of Ouled Berhil. More isolated, and somewhat less severe in hiking terms, than the Toubkal National Park *(see p.79)*, the Western Atlas offers some interesting possibilities, most of which are best organised in advance from Marrakesh.

At the top of the pass, the **Belle Vue Café**, see ⑪②, offers tea and panoramic views over the Souss plains to the Anti-Atlas Mountains, a more southern parallel range to the High Atlas.

On the south side, improvements to the road (wider bends and crash barriers) have made the Tizi-n-Test much less dangerous than it once was. That said, pay attention to oncoming trucks as you switchback down into the Souss. From the top of the pass it is 90km (56 miles) to Taroudant.

THE SOUSS VALLEY

After 37km (23 miles), turn right at the junction with the Ouarzazate–Agadir road and then continue a few kilometres into the rough-and-ready roadside town of **Ouled Berhil ❻**. There's not much of note here apart from a rather eccentric kasbah hotel set down a dusty left turn off the main drag. **Riad Hida** (tel: 0528-53 10 44; www.riadhida.com) offers 13 comfortable rooms and a pleasant garden with a pool, and makes a reasonable overnight stop. Otherwise, continue on through the **Souss Valley** (Vallée du Souss) to Taroudant, which

Unique Oil
The Souss Valley is also home to one of the world's rarer tree species – the argan. Only found in southern Morocco and in parts of Mexico, this thorny and rather unsightly species bears a nut that is used in the making of argan oil, used both in Moroccan cuisine and as a massage oil.

Food and Drink 🍴

② BELLE VUE CAFE
Summit of the Tizi-n-Test; no phone; open from 8am; $
This café/budget hotel, which offers some of the best views in Morocco from its terrace, makes an excellent stop for a refreshment break. There isn't a great deal of food on offer (just a handful of snacks), but they can rustle up an omelette, if you arrive in need of a meal. There is another café of the same name on the north side of the pass, but its views are not as good.

Above from left:
Taroudant's well-preserved city walls; olives at the souk; Agadir is Morocco's top beach resort; Taroudant musicians.

lies a further 44km (27 miles) west on the N10.

Oranges and Lemons

The fertile Souss is home to some of Morocco's largest producers of citrus fruit, much of which heads westwards to the port of Agadir for export. Along the main road you'll notice extensive orchards of oranges and lemons before you arrive in the walled city of Taroudant, which sits in the heart of the valley, in the shadow of some of the finest mountains in Morocco.

TAROUDANT

Taroudant ❼ is often likened to a miniature Marrakesh, and was also once a temporary seat of government prior to the capture of Marrakesh. Today, it is a compact and lively town, which, while rather short on monuments, boasts one of Morocco's most beautifully preserved city walls and some interesting souks. However, the city's medina bears few of the architectural

Below: details of the 19th-century Palais Salam Hotel.

treasures of Marrakesh: many of the buildings in the medina are modern breeze-block constructions that have superseded much of the architecture from centuries past.

The Souks

Apart from the rampart, the only historical site of any real interest is the impressive **Bab Kasbah**, a gateway into the city through the eastern wall. The souks themselves have become popular with visitors and now feature on many a coach-tour itinerary from the resort of Agadir. This has increased the city's hassle-factor, but there are still some unique crafts on offer as well as a couple of interesting antiques shops.

Staying Overnight

High rollers, royalty, heads of state and celebrities generally choose to stay at the very exclusive hideaway, **La Gazelle d'Or** (tel: 0528-85 20 39; www.gazelledor.com), tucked away out of time on the south side of the road to Amezgou. A more affordable option is the **Palais Salam Hotel** (tel: 028-85 25 01) on the eastern side of the city wall. This converted 19th-century palace of the then pasha has preserved much of its former splendour: the ground-floor bedrooms even enclose small, luxuriant gardens.

Taroudant is not big on restaurants, bars or nightlife, so you may decide to eat your evening meal in the hotel itself; otherwise, try the **Riad Dar Zitoune**, see ❶③, which also offers accommodation *(see p.115)*.

Food and Drink 🍴

③ RIAD DAR ZITOUNE
Boutariat El Berrania, Taroudant; tel: 028-55 11 41; open daily; $$–$$$
This hotel/restaurant, situated on the edge of town (on the road to Agadir), represents one of the best eating options in Taroudant. The restaurant boasts an international menu and guests can dine in an attractive poolside garden or in a vaulted dining room decorated in local style.

RETURN TO MARRAKESH

For those heading back to Marrakesh from Taroudant on day two, either retrace your journey back over the Tizi-n-Test, or take the geographically longer, although quicker and easier, route via Agadir on the Agadir–Marrakesh road, the N8. For the sake of variety you may elect to take this route to see some more of the country.

Agadir

Following a catastropic earthquake in 1960, **Agadir** ❽ was completely rebuilt and is now Morocco's premier beach resort, with 10km (6 miles) of broad sandy beach and an average of 300 days of sunshine a year. Conceived as a showcase for modern Morocco, it has no ancient medina or tempting souks, but it does have tourist shops, restaurants, hotels and international-style tourist complexes aplenty – and as many tourists as the rest of the country put together. One of the few remaining historic monuments is the **kasbah** – at the northern end of the bay – from which there are superb views down on to the port and the city.

Agadir is an example of full-throttle, commercial Morocco, but the city has a number of good restaurants on the seafront, which make it an ideal stop-off point before embarking on the 238km (149-mile) journey back to Marrakesh, which now only takes 2½ hours, since the new highway opened in 2010.

Sporting Life

Agadir offers a range of sporting possibilities, from golf at one of three well-kept courses to sea fishing, horse riding and a variety of water sports. For further information, the tourist office (tel: 028-84 63 77) can be found next to the Hotel Miramar on Avenue Mohammed V.

Below: Tafraoute.

Trips from Taroudant

Taroudant is often used as a springboard for trips further afield. For those with extra time on their hands there are several worthwhile excursions in the region, namely up into the Anti-Atlas Mountains and to the coast.

A strikingly scenic spot with a character all of its own, **Tafraoute** is located some 180km (112 miles) from Taroudant and can be visited as a two-day excursion. Highly recommended is a trip into the mountains, by way of the 'Paradise Valley', to the mountain village of **Imouzzèr-des-Ida-Outanane**, with its waterfall and the Hôtel des Cascades (tel: 0528-82 60 16). To find this road, which winds through picturesque palm oases and mountainside villages, take the coastal road northwards out of Agadir and turn right after 12km (7 miles). From here it is 49km (31 miles) up to the village and hotel. The following day, continue north out of the village until you rejoin the Agadir–Marrakesh road (N8). From the junction it takes about two-and-a-half hours back to Marrakesh along a fairly major route.

DIRECTORY

A user-friendly alphabetical listing of practical information, plus hand-picked hotels and restaurants, clearly organised by area, to suit all budgets and tastes. Selected nightlife listings are also included here.

A

ADMISSION CHARGES

These are very low, usually 10DH for an adult and often free for children. The Majorelle Garden and the Ben Youssef Madrassa have higher charges, but these are inexpensive by European standards.

AGE RESTRICTIONS

You must be over 21 to hire a car in Morocco, and over 16 to buy alcohol.

B

BUDGETING

Accommodation: An average price for a double room in a reasonable-quality hotel/riad will cost around 1,000-1,500DH, perhaps a little less in high season (mid-summer), but you can stay in a clean but basic hotel for 300DH or less.

Eating Out: A three-course meal for two with Moroccan wine in a mid-range restaurant will cost about 600DH; a coffee about 20DH; and a beer 40–60DH depending on the venue. You can eat in a good but basic grill restaurant for about 150DH for two.

Transport: Hiring a small car for a week costs from around DH3,500. Hiring a *grand taxi* and driver for the day costs around 800DH, depending on distance, often more if organised through your hotel.

C

CHILDCARE

Moroccans are very welcoming of children, including in restaurants; however, that may not be the case in some of the foreign-owned riads, so be sure to check this when you book. Nappies and formula milk are widely available, usually in grocery shops rather than pharmacies. However, to be sure of getting your usual brand you should bring these items with you. Some of the larger hotels offer babysitting services.

CLIMATE

The best times to be in Marrakesh are late autumn and early spring. Winter is usually bright and sunny, and sometimes warm enough to swim, but it can also be cold, especially at night when temperatures can drop to below freezing. Mid-summer is usually too hot for comfort as temperatures average 33°C (91°F) and top 40°C (104°F). Summer visitors will need a hotel with air-conditioning and preferably a pool.

CLOTHING

In summer pack light cottons; in winter be sure to take both light clothes for daytime and warm clothing (including a coat) for the evening.

Also remember that Morocco is an Islamic country and don't wear revealing clothes on the streets. In the evenings, smart-casual is acceptable for most venues. You won't get into some

of the more exclusive hotels, including La Mamounia, wearing jeans.

CRIME

Crime is not especially common, but you should take the usual precautions: use a safe in your hotel; don't carry too much cash on you; keep an eye on bags and valuables; and don't leave belongings visible in a parked car. At night be sure to park your car in a guarded car park.

If you are the victim of crime, you will need to report it to the police (there is a Tourist Police station on the north side of the Jemaa el Fna) and obtain an official report to present to your insurer upon your return.

It is inadvisable to buy or use hashish. There are many Westerners languishing in Moroccan prisons for drug offences.

CUSTOMS

The airport Duty Free shop is open to incoming as well as departing passengers. Passengers can import 1 litre of alcohol (wine or spirits); 200 cigarettes or 50 cigarillos or 25 cigars; 150ml of perfume or 250ml of toilet water; and gifts up to a value of 2,000DH. You may not import or export dirhams: all local currency must be exchanged in Morocco.

D

DISABLED TRAVELLERS

Disabled access is generally not good in Morocco. High kerbs in the New Town and uneven surfaces in the medina make wheelchair use difficult, and most of the museums occupy old palaces or riads with maze-like layouts and lots of steps. Even when restaurants are accessible, the toilets are rarely so. That said, Moroccans are quick to assist where they can.

DRIVING

It is not worth hiring a car for getting around Marrakesh, as taxis are so cheap, and many places are inaccessible by car; it is worth it, however, if you want to get out and see the surrounding region, which is spectacular (especially in the cases of Routes 11–14). However, if you only want to go to Essaouira you are probably better off getting the Supratours bus or the CTM bus, both of which are cheap and efficient (see p.66).

Car Hire

You can book car hire in advance from home using one of the international companies. However, it is often cheaper to arrange something *in situ*; most companies have offices around Place Abdel Moumen Ben Ali on Avenue Mohammed V. Do try haggling, especially for longer periods. Aside from the usual international companies, such as Avis, Hertz and Europcar, which all have local offices, try these local operators:

Florida: tel: 0524-44 42 18; 28 Rue Koutoubia, Marrakech.
Sweet Tour: tel: 0524-43 88 34; www. sweet-tour.com.

Above from far left: rooftop view of the city; Berber child; flags of state bearing Morocco's five-pointed star; *grands taxis* are usually large cream Mercedes.

Self-Drive
To bring your own car into Morocco you will need Green Card insurance (this can be purchased on arrival at the port in Tangier if your own insurance company doesn't provide it for Morocco), your vehicle registration document and a European-style photocard licence or international licence.

Rules of the Road

Speed limits are: 40kph (25mph) in urban areas, 100kph (60mph) on the open road, and 120kph (74mph) on motorways (but look out for signs specifying other limits). Be careful to observe these limits: speed-traps are common, especially on approaches to towns. You will receive a small on-the-spot fine for breaking the speed limit. You may also be stopped if front-seat passengers are not wearing a seatbelt.

The old French system of *priorité à droite* (right of way to traffic coming from the right, ie vehicles on a round-about give way to vehicles coming on to it) is being phased out. However, it is still the case on some round-abouts, so be sure to approach them with care.

As a rule, Moroccans drive quite chaotically but slowly. Dangerous overtaking on main roads is common, so again be cautious.

Breakdown

Your car-hire company should provide you with the number of their breakdown company. Otherwise, flag down a fellow driver and ask for a lift to a repair garage in the nearest town to get assistance.

Parking

Your riad or hotel will be able to advise on parking. If they don't have their own car park, you will need to park in a public carpark or on the street. Either way, a *gardien*, who wears an official badge, will keep an eye on your car for a small charge (3–4DH is sufficient for

an hour or two, but overnight parking usually costs 15–20DH).

E

ELECTRICITY

The electricity supply is rated 220 volts in all but the very oldest hotels. Plugs are the round two-pin Continental type, so bring an adaptor if you want to use UK or US appliances.

EMBASSIES/CONSULATES

Moroccan Embassies
UK
49 Queen's Gate Gardens, London SW7 5NE; tel: 020-7581 5001.

US
1601 21st Street NW, Washington, DC 20009; tel: 202-462 7979; http://dcusa.themoroccanembassy.com.

Moroccan Consulate
US
10 East 40th Street, Floor 23, New York, NY 10016; tel: 212-758 2625; www.moroccanconsulate.com.

Embassies in Morocco
British Embassy
28 Avenue SAR Sidi Mohammed, Rabat; tel: 0537-63 33 33; www.british embassy.gov.uk.

US Embassy
2 Avenue de Marrakech, Rabat; tel: 0537-76 22 65; http://rabat.us embassy.gov.

Petrol Tips

Petrol stations are plentiful except on routes through the Atlas, where you should be sure to fill up in advance. Forecourt attendants normally fill the tank for you, and may also clean your windscreen and headlamps (small tip welcome but not essential). Most hire cars take lead-free *(sans plomb)*, which is widely available, but be sure to check when you take charge of the car. Petrol costs slightly less than in the UK; more than in the US.

EMERGENCIES

Emergency telephone numbers are:
Police: **19**
Fire service/ambulance: **15**
There is an office of the Tourist Police on the north side of the Jemaa el Fna.

ETIQUETTE

In the interests of tourism, *Marrakshis* are fairly tolerant of the behaviour of foreigners, but it is polite to be respectful of Morocco's Muslim culture and avoid wearing revealing clothes in the medina or indulging in overt displays of physical affection (although holding hands is fine). During Ramadan try to avoid eating on the streets in daylight hours.

Non-Muslims cannot enter working mosques in Morocco.

F

FESTIVALS

The festival calendar is getting busier year on year, as new festivals are added to boost year-round interest in the city. Some of the main ones are:
January: The Marrakesh Marathon; www.marathon-marrakech.com.
March: Riad Art Expo – art festival staged in the city's many riads; www.riadart-expo.com.
June: Essaouira's Gnaoua Music Festival takes over the town *(see p.71)*; www.festival-gnaoua.net.
July: The Festival National des Arts Populaires de Marrakech takes place at

El Badi Palace, celebrating local folklore; www.marrakechfestival.com.
December: International Film Festival – held in early December in the Palais des Congrès, the Théâtre Royal and various smaller venues. A giant screen is erected on the Jemaa el Fna's western side; www.festivalmarrakech.info.

G

GAY TRAVELLERS

Homosexuality is, in theory, illegal, and can incur a prison sentence of three months to three years. It is therefore important to approach gay encounters with Moroccans with caution; it could be a set-up or there may be an economic motive. That said, Marrakesh has long been a centre for expatriate male homosexuality, and many foreign-owned riads offer discreet places to stay.

H

HEALTH

No vaccinations are required for entry into Morocco unless you have come from a yellow fever, cholera or smallpox zone. If you need to see a doctor or dentist during your stay in Morocco, staff in your hotel/riad will be able to assist in finding one.

Insurance
All medical care must be paid for so be sure to take out adequate health insurance before you travel.

Ramadan and the Traveller
The Muslim month of fasting has some disadvantages for travellers. Certainly, restaurants and cafés are much quieter during the day (some even close for the month) and some restaurants that normally sell alcohol do not during this time.

Stomach Upsets

These are easily avoided, if a few simple precautions are taken: don't eat food that has been left standing or reheated, peel fruit, treat salads with circumspection and only drink bottled water. If you are struck down, drink plenty of water, preferably with rehydration salts, and take a diarrhoea remedy (available at pharmacies).

HOURS AND HOLIDAYS

Business Hours

Shops in the medina: Sat–Thur 10am–8pm, some also open Fri.
Shops in Guéliz: Mon–Sat 10am–1.30pm and 3.30–7.30pm, closed Sun.
Banks: Winter: Mon–Fri 8.30am–11.30am and 2.30–4pm; summer: Mon–Fri 8.30–11.30am and 3–5pm; Ramadan: Mon–Fri 9.30am–3pm.

State Holidays

New Year's Day: 1 Jan
Independence Manifesto Day: 11 Jan
Labour Day: 1 May
Feast of the Throne: 30 July
Act of Allegiance: 14 Aug
Revolution Day: 20 Aug
Youth Day: 21 Aug
Anniversary of the Green March: 6 Nov
Independence Day: 18 Nov

Muslim Holidays

These are governed by the Hegira lunar calendar and are therefore movable. The holidays get earlier by 11 days each year (12 in a leap year).

Exact dates depend on the sighting of the new moon.
Mouloud: The Prophet's birthday. In 2011 this falls on 15 Feb.
Aid es Seghir: (marking the end of Ramadan). 30 Aug in 2011.
Aid el Kebir: (feast of Abraham's sacrifice of a lamb instead of his son). 7 Nov in 2011.
Muslim New Year: 26 Nov in 2011.

I

INTERNET

There are numerous internet cafés and some of the *téléboutiques* also offer internet access. The Cyber Parc at the foot of Avenue Mohammed V has internet booths scattered around the park as well as an indoor internet station. Internet access costs around 8–10DH an hour; many of the better hotels offer WiFi.

L

LANGUAGE

Moroccans speak their own dialect of Arabic, but written communication is in classical Arabic. There are also various Berber dialects, and in the Marrakesh region it 0is *chleuh*. Although most Berbers understand Arabic, few Arabs understand Berber.

French is also widely spoken and understood, although fluency is not as widespread as it used to be, partly because children are no longer taught in French in state schools.

Picture Perfect

Morocco has served as a location for many famous films, from Orson Welles's *Othello* (Essaouira, 1952) to *The Bourne Ultimatum* (Tangier, 2007). Among the films specifically made in Marrakesh are *The Man Who Knew Too Much* (1956), *Hideous Kinky* (1998), *The Mummy* (1999) and *Sex in the City 2* (2010). Plenty more have been made in the Atlas Mountains *(see p.87)*.

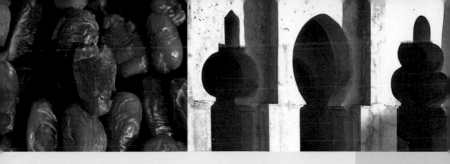

Useful Phrases in Arabic

Hello *Márhaba, ahlan*

Welcome *Ahlan wa sahlan*

Good morning *Sbah l-khir*

Good evening *Msa l-khir*

Goodbye *Beslama*

How are you? *La bas?*

I'm fine *Labas*

Please *'Afak*

Thank you *Shukran*

Yes/No *Iyyeh/Lla*

What's your name? *Ashnu smitek?*

My name is… *Smiti…*

Where are you from? *Mnin nta?* (to a man); *mnin nti?* (to a woman)

I'm from England/the US *Ana men inglatirra/amrika*

Do you speak English/French? *Wash kat-kellem l-ingliziya/l-fransawiya?*

I don't understand *Ma f-hemt-sh*

What does this mean? *Ashnu kat'ni hadi?* (for feminine); *Ashnu kay'ni hada?* (for masculine)

Never mind *Ma'alish*

It's forbidden *Mamnu'*

What time is it? *Shal f sa'a?*

Emergencies

I need help *Bghit musa'ada*

Hospital *Sbitar*

Pharmacy *Farmasyan*

Diarrhoea *S-haal*

Police *Bolis*

Getting Around

Where? *Feen?*

Downtown *Wust l-mdina*

Taxi *Taxi*

Grand/shared taxi *Taxi kbir*

Aeroplane *Tiyyara*

Station *Mahatta, la station*

To/From *Al/Men*

Right/Left *Limen/Lsser*

MAPS

A free and up-to-date map is distributed by the tourist office *(see p.107)*, but its coverage of the complex souk area is sketchy.

In addition to the map found in the back of this book, the best available maps are *Insight FlexiMap Marrakesh*, published by Apa Publications; *Marrakech & Essaouira* published by Editions Laure Kane; and Michelin map no. 742, which covers the whole of Morocco and features an enlargement of Marrakesh.

In the UK, these are most easily available from the travel book and map specialist Stanfords (12–14 Long Acre, London WC2, and 29 Corn Street, Bristol BS2; www.stanfords.co.uk; orders can be placed online), as well as other good bookshops.

MEDIA

Publications

There is a range of daily and weekly publications in French and Arabic. The two main publications in French are the pro-Royal *Le Matin* and the more liberal *L'Opinion*. Weeklies include *Le Journal* and the outspoken *TelQuel*. *Le Monde* is also widely available, as are some English newspapers, but the latter will be at least a day old by the time you buy them.

Above from far left: lamplit restaurant doorway; young Moroccans; dates; detail from the Koubbal el Baroudiyn, the only Almoravid building left in the city.

Local Cure
A local remedy for upset stomachs is cactus fruit, also known as Barbary fig. You will see it being sold from stands on street corners. For a few dirhams the vendor will peel one or two for you while you wait.

For listings of forthcoming events consult the monthly *Couleurs Marrakech*, available in hotel and restaurant foyers.

Television

Most hotels provide CNN and BBC World satellite channels. Morocco has two state-run TV channels, 2M and TVM, which are more interesting than they used to be, providing that you can understand French or Arabic, but far from essential viewing. It also operates two privately run satellite channels, Al Maghribiya and Mid 1 Sat.

MONEY

Moroccan dirhams (DH) cannot be imported or exported, which means that they cannot be obtained in advance of your trip. On departure you can change unspent dirhams back into hard currency in the airport but you must show exchange receipts totalling twice the amount you want to change back, as well as your flight boarding card.

The dirham is a reasonably stable currency. Recent exchange rates have hovered around 15DH to £1 sterling, 11DH to €1, and 9DH to $1. Rates vary between banks, so shop around.

ATMs

ATMs are the easiest way of obtaining cash, although your bank may charge you a handling fee as well as interest if you are using a credit card (you can often use debit cards bearing the Cirrus logo, but don't rely on this alone). ATMs are plentiful in the New Town and there are a couple of Banque Populaire ATMs at

the top of Rue Bab Agnaou, off the Jemaa el Fna. The daily limit on withdrawals is currently 2,000DH.

Credit Cards

MasterCard and Visa are accepted in most hotels, petrol stations and the more expensive shops and restaurants. Other cards are less widely accepted.

POLICE

Most matters concerning tourists are handled by the Tourist Police, who have a station on the northern side of the Jemaa el Fna (tel: 0524-38 46 01).

POST

The main post office (PTT) is on Place 16 Novembre in Guéliz. Stamps are available from tobacconists.

RELIGION

Islam

Morocco is a comparatively tolerant Muslim country, but religion is still the biggest influence on society. The five requirements of Islam – affirmation that there is no other god but God and Mohammed is his Prophet; prayer five times a day; the observance of Ramadan; the giving of alms to the poor; and making the *hadj* (pilgrimage) to Mecca at least once in a lifetime – are central to many Moroccan lives.

Officially, Morocco follows the Sunni (orthodox) branch of Islam. However, there are many thriving Sufi brotherhoods that promote a more mystical approach to God.

Christianity

Marrakesh has a small Christian community. They are served by the little Catholic church in Guéliz *(see p.55)*.

T

TELEPHONES

Phone booths, mainly run by Maroc Telecom, are plentiful. They are operated with phone cards sold at tobacconists. In addition you will find *téleboutiques* where you can use coins and get change from the attendant.

To make an international call, dial 00 for an international line, followed by the country code (44 for the UK). Remember to drop the initial zero of the UK area code you are dialling.

TIME

Morocco keeps to Greenwich Mean Time all year round. It is one hour behind UK time during summer and the same time as the UK in winter.

TIPPING

It is usual to tip porters, chambermaids, other hotel staff if they are particularly helpful, and waiting staff. There are no hard-and-fast rules for the amount: 10 percent would be considered generous.

TOURIST INFORMATION

The main tourist office is on Place Abdel Moumen Ben Ali in Guéliz (tel: 0524-43 61 79). It is open Mon–Fri 8.30am noon and 2.30-6.30pm, Sat 9am–noon and 3-6pm.

TOURS

There are countless local companies offering a wide range of tours, from short guided tours in Marrakesh to excursions into the Atlas and southern Morocco. Two reputable companies are: **Ribat Tours** (6 Rue des Vieux Marrakchis, Guéliz; tel: 0524-43 86 93; www.ribatours.com), which specialises in outdoor activities, and **Terres et Voyages** (Immeuble D1, 8 Avenue 11 Janvier, Bab Doukkala; tel: 0524-43 71 53; www.terresetvoyages.com), a reliable mainstream tour operator, that has an English-speaking owner.

TRANSPORT

Arrival by Air

Royal Air Maroc operates a daily flight to Marrakesh from London Heathrow via Casablanca. Sometimes this involves a long delay in Casablanca while waiting for connecting flights from other countries in Europe.

Royal Air Maroc in the UK: Langham House, 32–33 Gosfield Street, London W1; tel: 020-7307 5800; www.royalairmaroc.com.

Royal Air Maroc in Marrakesh: 197 Avenue Mohammed V; tel: 0524-42 55 01; www.royalairmaroc.com.

Above from far left: fresh fruit seller; shop around for the best bank exchange rate.

Marrakesh is well served by the following budget airlines:

Atlas Blue (www.royalairmaroc.com) is the budget arm of Royal Air Maroc, flying out of London Gatwick.

Other budget airlines with services from the UK to Marrakesh are **easy-Jet** (www.easyjet.com) flying from London Gatwick; **Ryanair** (www.ryanair.com) from London Luton; and **Thomson Fly** (http://flights.thomson.co.uk) from London Gatwick and Manchester.

Arrival by Train

It is possible to travel to Marrakesh by train via Paris (Eurostar to Gare du Nord and then change to Gare d'Austerlitz) for Algeciras, where ferries leave for Tangier throughout the day. From Tangier there are three day-time trains to Marrakesh (journey time 9–10 hours), but you're best off booking a couchette on the overnight train, which leaves daily at 9.05pm and arrives at 8.05am.

In Tangier you will need to take a taxi from the ferry terminal to the railway station as they are at opposite ends of the bay. The first-class couchettes accommodate four passengers in each compartment, and although not luxurious, are comfortable enough. There is normally only one couchette carriage so it is advisable to book your place in advance. Check out schedules and fares on www.oncf.ma.

Arrival by Road

After taking the ferry from Algeciras to Tangier, it is a 600km (370-mile)

drive along the new and wonderfully deserted toll motorway to Marrakesh.

Airport

Upon arrival you will be required to fill out an immigration form before going through passport control. The arrivals hall has the usual facilities, including a bank and cash machine, and car-hire firms. There are two terminals (and a third one to open in 2012): terminal 2 handles all of the budget airlines.

On departure you will also need to fill out an immigration form before passing through passport control. The café in the departure lounge will take euros as well as dirhams.

From the Airport. Marrakech-Menara Airport is situated 6km (4 miles) from the city centre. There is normally a plentiful supply of taxis outside the terminal. The fare into town should be no more than 80–100DH, although you will probably be asked for about 200DH in the first instance so be prepared to bargain. Drivers will accept euros if you do not have dirhams. There is also an irregular bus service (no. 11) to the Jemaa el Fna every 30 minutes or so.

Transport within Marrakesh

Taxis. There are two types of taxi in Morocco: *petits taxis* (greeny-beige livery) and *grands taxis* (large cream Mercedes).

Petits taxis take up to three passengers and can be hired on the street. Fares are very cheap, but drivers usually refuse to use the meter so you must

Mobile Phones
To use your own mobile phone in Morocco you should check costs with your own mobile-phone company before leaving home. Alternatively, you can buy a prepaid mobile phone while in Morocco or buy a SIM card for use in your own phone. These are available from Maroc Telecom or Meditel, which have outlets all over the place.

negotiate a set price before you embark. It is not unusual for people to share *petits taxis*, so don't be surprised if your driver picks up another passenger along the way.

Grands taxis take up to six passengers. You can charter a *grand taxi* for the day or for a longer trip (easily arranged through your hotel, or more cheaply by negotiating directly with drivers at the *grands-taxis* stations). In Guéliz the main station is next door to the train station on Avenue Hassan II.

City Buses. There is a good bus service, although buses can get very crowded. One of the most useful buses for tourists is the no. 1 from Place de Foucauld to Place Abdel Moumen Ben Ali. Other useful routes are nos 2 and 10 for the bus station, and nos 3 and 8 for the train station. The flat fare on all buses is 3.5DH. Payment is made upon boarding; drivers will supply change for smaller notes.

Calèches. Horse-drawn carriages congregate outside the larger hotels and at various points around the city, most notably opposite Club Med on Place de Foucauld. Official prices are posted inside the calèche but be sure to check the price with the driver before boarding *(see also p.64)*.

Trains. The entrance to Marrakesh's train station is on Avenue Mohammed VI. The station runs direct services to Casablanca, Rabat, Fez, Tangier and Meknès. For information: tel: 090-20 30 40; www.oncf.ma.

Long-Distance Bus/Coach Travel.
Supratours (tel: 0524-47 53 17; www. supratourstravel.com) and CTM (tel: 0524-43 44 02; www.ctm.ma) are the most useful companies. The Supratours office is on Avenue Hassan II, next door to the *grands taxis* and railway stations.

VISAS AND PASSPORTS

Holders of full British passports or American passports can enter Morocco for a stay of up to three months without a visa, but their passport must be valid for at least six months after the planned departure date.

WEBSITES

www.tourism-in-morocco.com
The national tourist office.
www.maroc.net
News, culture and useful information.
www.terremaroc.com
Tourist information site. Particularly good for finding riad accommodation.

WOMEN TRAVELLERS

Women travellers do receive a low level of harassment, but this usually remains a mild irritant rather than anything more threatening. Keep hassle to a minimum by behaving coolly but courteously, wearing modest clothing and avoiding eye contact.

Above from far left: you need a phone card to use a phone booth; the main post office in Guéliz.

The Medina

Les Borjs de la Kasbah

Rue du Méchouar; tel: 0524-38 11 01; www.lesborjsdelakasbah.com; $$$

This comfortable hotel was converted from an old riad. It is located in the upper reaches of the Kasbah area. Spacious double and superior rooms (some singles available) situated around a series of courtyards. Facilities include a good little restaurant, a heated pool secluded by high red walls, and a hammam in one of the watchtowers. Special offers often available in low season.

Casa Lalla

16 Derb Jemaa, off Rue Riad Zitoun el Kdim; tel: 0524-42 97 57; www.casalalla.com; $$

This is a stylish riad with a good position in the southern part of the medina. It is worth coming here for the food alone (there is a 'tasting dinner' at 8pm every evening, also open to non-residents), and the eight rooms, each with its own special feature (such as a private terrace, fireplace or mezzanine sleeping area), are comfortably and tastefully furnished, all with chic and luxurious bathrooms.

Price for a double room for one night in high season, usually includes breakfast unless otherwise stated:

$$$$	over 2,500DH
$$$	1,600–2,500DH
$$	700–1,600DH
$	under 700DH

Dar Warda

266 Derb Sidi Bouamor, Riad Laarous; tel: 0524-37 83 56; www.darwarda.com; $$

This is a small, intimate and tastefully furnished riad. It comprises just five attractive rooms set around a central patio. The riad is located in the northern half of the medina.

Dar More

44 Derb Jdid. Rue Riad Zitoun el Kdim; tel: 0524-661 39 86 20; www.riad-dar-more.com; $$

Just five minute's walk from Jemaa el Fna is this charming and entirely rebuilt riad. It is a calm oasis in the centre of the busy city, having been furnished with contemporary flair by its stylish French owner, Dominique. In addition, it offers excellent value, and does good breakfasts.

Hotel Essaouira

3 Sidi Bouloukate; tel: 0524-44 38 05; $

Rock-bottom prices (just 100DH a night for a double) and a good location near the Jemaa el Fna make this a popular choice for budget travellers. It is centrally located and the rooms are bright and clean. Essential to book in advance. Like many of the good-value places listed here, they do not accept credit cards.

Hotel de Foucauld

Avenue el Mouahidine; tel: 0524-44 54 99; $

This older-style hotel has a gloomy exterior, has lost a star and is no longer

licensed (it still allows customers to bring their own alcohol), but it is conveniently located just a stone's throw from the Jemaa el Fna, and remains a firm favourite among hikers and adventure travellers. Like some other places, they don't accept credit cards.

Hotel Gallia

30 Rue de la Recette; tel: 0524-44 59 13; $

Attractive and comfortable rooms are arranged around a traditionally tiled courtyard with a palm tree in the middle. Well situated off Rue Bab Agnaou near the Jemaa el Fna. Book well ahead.

Hotel Sherazade

Derb Riad Zitoun el Kdim; tel: 0524-42 93 05; www.hotelsherazade.com; $

Popular small hotel (22 rooms), based around two riads with plant-filled courtyards and good rooftop terraces. Some rooms have air-conditioning and some shared facilities, but most are en-suite.

Riad Farnatchi

2 Derb el Farnatchi; tel: 0524-384910; www.riadfarnatchi.com; $$$$

This movie-star-fabulous riad is an exercise in discreet luxury. The nine suites are sumptuously huge yet cosy, with sunken baths and terraces where you can eat your breakfast to the sound of birdsong. Lynn Perez and her team are breathtakingly efficient and helpful. A place to stay that earns every DH of its price tag.

Les Jardins de la Medina

Derb Chtouka; tel: 0524-38 18 51; www.lesjardinsdelamedina.com; $$$$

A huge riad converted into a comfortable hotel with a walled garden, pool and hammam, and a notable restaurant. The decor is modern Moorish with clean lines and bold designs. Most rooms have a fireplace, and superior rooms also have a terrace. It is, however, a good 15-minute walk from the Jemaa el Fna.

La Maison Arabe

1 Derb Assehbe; tel: 0524-38 70 10; www.lamaisonarabe.com; $$$$

This hotel near Bab Doukkala started out as a restaurant, and its well-regarded cookery workshops are part of its success. The standard rooms are good value, especially in low season, while the superior rooms have fireplaces and terraces. There's no on-site pool, but a shuttle bus will take guests to one 10 minutes away if they like. Rates include afternoon tea as well as breakfast.

Riad el Fenn

Bab el Ksour; tel: 0524-44 12 10; www.riadelfenn.com; $$$$

Co-owned by Richard Branson's wife, this happens to be one of the medina's most chic and exclusive riads, with modern art on the walls and secluded areas for lounging. Facilities include a screening room (used during the city's International Film Festival) and an 18m (60ft) long putting green, as well as a superb pool and hammam.

Above from far left: the heated pool at Les Borjs de la Kasbah; ornate door handle at La Sultana (see p.112), Riyad el Cadi (see p.112); a warm welcome.

Fancy a Riad?
If your heart is set on staying in a riad, be aware that they vary tremendously, from a simple guesthouse with two or three rooms to stylish boutique hotels offering every luxury. There are several websites that specialise in booking riad accommodation; you can normally book a room, suite or a whole riad. For a range of riads in the northern part of the medina, try Marrakech Riads (tel: 0524-39 16 09; www.marrakech-riads.net).

Riad Magi

79 Derb Moulay Abdel Kader, Dabachi; tel: 0524-42 66 88; www.riad-magi.com; $$

Attractive and intimate riad, situated east of the main souks, with six en-suite rooms in strong North African colour schemes. There is also a pleasant roof terrace. Breakfast is included, and other meals can be ordered by arrangement.

Riad l'Orangerie

61 Rue Sidi el-Yamani; tel: 0524-661 238 789; www.riadorangerie.com; $$

With great staff, tranquil atmosphere, good breakfasts and rooms in pale colours decorated in sparse Moroccan style and set around a courtyard with a swimming pool, this is one of the medina's most sought-after addresses.

Riad Safar

29 Derb Ouihah, Quartier Sidi Abdelaziz; tel: 0524-39 10 10; $$

This four-room riad is decorated in sumptuous traditional style and is a peaceful haven tucked away in the medina, a short walk from the Jemaa el Fna. Staff are helpful and welcoming. Recommended.

> Price for a double room for one night in high season, usually includes breakfast unless otherwise stated:
>
> $$$$ over 2,500DH
> $$$ 1,600–2,500DH
> $$ 700–1,600DH
> $ under 700DH

Riyad el Cadi

87 Derb Moulay Abdelkader, Dabachi; tel: 0524-37 86 55; www.riyadelcadi.com; $$$

This large riad just east of the main souks comprises 12 rooms or suites leading off five patios. The rooms feature antique textiles, and there is a small pool and a pleasant roof terrace. The self-contained Blue House, which is equipped with its own kitchen and patio, is ideal for private hire. Meals can be ordered.

La Sultana

403 Rue de la Kasbah; tel: 0524-38 80 08; www.lasultanamarrakech. com; $$$$

Ornate luxury hotel with a good location near the Saadian Tombs. A complex of four riads offers 28 spacious rooms and suites, an attractive heated pool, and a well-equipped spa with an open-air jacuzzi on its roof. A little over the top for many people's taste but the very definition of oriental for others.

Villa des Orangers

6 Rue Sidi Mimoun; tel: 0524-38 46 38; www.villadesorangers.com; $$$$

Established hotel that successfully incorporates modern comforts (large, sleek beds and luxuriously appointed bathrooms) in a traditional but tasteful setting with antique furniture, open fires in winter, a good-size pool and excellent restaurant. One of the city's top addresses, and not far from the Jemaa el Fna.

Villa Flore

4 Derb Azzouz; tel: 0524-39 17 00;
www.villa-flore.com; $$

A small boutique hotel that is well located in the Mouassine quarter in the northern medina. Villa Flore's five rooms are individually furnished in a fresh, modern style, and have well-equipped bathrooms. The hotel also has a good restaurant, and half-board terms are available.

Guéliz and the Hivernage

Hotel Diwane

Rue de Yougoslavie; tel: 0524-43 22 16; www.diwane-hotel.com; $$

A no-frills, reasonably priced four-star hotel just off Place Abdel Moumen Ben Ali in the centre of the New Town, with decent-sized rooms and a good pool. Ideal for families.

Hotel Le Grand Imilchil

Avenue Echouhada, Hivernage; tel: 0524-44 76 53; $

One of the older 1970s-built hotels, located between the medina and Guéliz. It is efficiently run, the rooms are large and there is a nice pool. No alcohol.

Hotel La Mamounia

Avenue Bab Jdid; tel: 0524-38 86 00; www.mamounia.com; $$$$

This former palace, which was turned into a hotel in 1923, has now finished the massive refurbishment funded by the king. It is anticipated that the new-look hotel will restore its reputation as the premier place to stay, with elegantly designed rooms and suites, all exceptionally luxurious, and the revamped public areas beautifully finished. Its gardens, casino and piano bar are open to non-residents *(see p.62)*.

The Palmeraie

Les Deux Tours

Douar Abiad; tel: 0524-32 95 25; www.les-deuxtours.com; $$$$

A plush hotel spread out across beautiful gardens in the Palmeraie, with a good pool and hammam. The architecture is Moroccan-traditional. It is a favourite among fashion photographers, and more affordable than some of the private villas nearby.

Jnane Tamsna

Douar Abiad; tel: 0524-32 93 40; www.jnanetamsna.com; $$$$

Set in beautiful grounds, the luxurious Jnane Tamsna complex is comprised of spacious and beautifully furnished rooms and suites in three guesthouses plus a gorgeous new hotel. Amenities include two pools, an opulent salon, tennis courts and lush gardens, where organic produce for the kitchen is grown.

Palmeraie Golf Palace

Circuit de la Palmeraie; tel: 0524-36 87 04/22/23; www.pgpmarrakech.com; $$$$+

Vast luxury complex (with eight restaurants, five pools, a fitness centre and horse riding) attached to superb 18-hole golf course. Also hosts Nikki Beach *(see p.60)* and Dar Ennasim restaurant *(see p.120)*, run by chef Fabrice Vulin.

Above from far left: Riad Magi; Villa des Orangers.

Outskirts of Marrakesh

Amanjena

Route de Ouarzazate, km 12; tel: 0524-40 35 53; www.amanjena. com; $$$$

The first Aman resort in Africa is situated 12km (7 miles) south of Marrakesh on the Ouarzazate road. The ultimate in luxury, it comprises palatial pavilions set among palm and olive trees, some with their own pool and butler service. Every amenity you could desire, at similarly exalted prices.

Villas Fawakay

Off Route de Ouarzazate, km 8; tel: 0673 18 73 46; www.villasfawakay. com; $$$

Hidden away down a dusty road, this unusual place, run by an English expat family who live on site, consists of three large, stylish villas in verdant gardens with a pool. It combines privacy with the ease of a hotel, as meals are all catered for – there's a nightly menu of delicious dishes.

Essaouira

Palais Heure Bleu

2 Rue Ibn Batouta; tel: 0524-78 34 34; www.heure-bleu.com; $$$$

Price for a double room for one night in high season, usually includes breakfast unless otherwise stated:

$$$$	over 2,500DH
$$$	1,600–2,500DH
$$	700–1,600DH
$	under 700DH

Essaouira's finest hotel has gracious rooms and suites that are beautifully decorated in styles bearing African, oriental and British colonial influences. There is a stunning rooftop pool with views over the city, a private cinema, a billiard room and a spa that includes a massage room with wraparound views.

Riad Loulema

2 Rue Souss; tel: 0524-47 53 46; www.darloulema.com; $$

A bright and cosy riad that is built against the ramparts and has eight individually decorated rooms with en-suite facilities. Breakfast is served on the shady terrace or the patio. The pleasant staff are pleased to help in whatever way they can to make your stay enjoyable.

Villa Maroc

10 Rue Abdellah Ben Yassine; tel: 0524-47 31 47; www.villa-maroc. com; $$–$$$

One of the first riad-style guesthouses to open in Morocco, Villa Maroc remains one of the nicest places to stay in Essaouira. It offers lovely rooms with fireplaces and tiled floors, a leafy terrace, good food and a restful environment, including a hammam. Excellent location not far from the main square, and with views over the seafront.

Imlil, Mount Toubkal, Tizi-n-Test, Taroudant

La Bergerie

Ouirgane; tel: 0524-48 57 17; www.labergerie-maroc.ma; $$

This stone lodge decorated in traditional Berber style is situated amidst some outstanding countryside. It offers simple but comfortable rooms (some with fireplace), a cosy restaurant and bar, and an outdoor pool in summer.

Dar Imlil

Imlil; tel: 061-69 27 65; www.kasbah dutoubkal.com; $$–$$$

This small hotel is set in some lovely countryside some 10 minutes from the centre of Imlil. They have a great terrace overlooking the valley, and simple but comfortable rooms with en-suite facilities.

Domaine de la Roseraie

Ouirgane; tel: 0524-43 91 28; www.laroseraiehotel.com; $$$

Long-established mountain retreat (40 rooms and four suites, the latter with their own fireplaces) set in the midst of lovely gardens. There is a good restaurant, plus three pools and a hammam, and horse riding and trekking with mules can be arranged.

Kasbah Tamadot

Route d'Imlil; tel: 0524-36 82 00; www.kasbahtamadot.virgin.com; $$$$

Kasbah-style luxury retreat owned by Richard Branson, with lovely views towards Mount Toubkal. The accommodation ranges from affordable doubles to considerably more expensive suites and Berber tented suites. Facilities include indoor and outdoor pools, an ultra-luxurious hammam, a superb restaurant, and much more besides (see

also p.78). You can also go trekking by mule from here.

Kasbah du Toubkal

Imlil; tel: 0524-48 56 11; www. kasbahdutoubkal.com; $–$$$$

Converted kasbah with eco-friendly credentials and outstanding views over the Toubkal massif. Offers a range of lodging options, from inexpensive dormitory accommodation to a luxury apartment. Bookings are only taken for two days or longer. (See also p.80.)

Riad Dar Zitoune

Boutarial El Berrania, Taroudant; tel: 028-55 11 41; www.darzitoune.com; $$–$$$

An attractively rustic option, with a mix of Berber and Moorish decor, and a nice pool set in a verdant garden. Offers a range of rooms and suites. (See also p.96.)

Tizi-n-Tichka, Ouarzazate

Dar Daïf

Talmasla, Ouarzazate; tel: 0524-85 42 32/47; www.dardaif.ma; $$

An excellent small hotel located 5km (3 miles) outside the town and offering a hammam and pool, plus individually decorated rooms.

Dar Qamar

Kasbah Agdz, Agdz; tel: 0524-84 37 84; www.locsudmaroc.com; $$–$$$

A corner of the Agdz Kasbah that is now a mid-range hotel with comfortable if simply furnished rooms, a restaurant and pool. There's also an attractive tented area for lounging under the stars in the evening. (See also p.89.)

Above from far left: Palmeraie Golf Palace; Dar Qamar.

The Medina

Dar Moha

81 Rue Dar el Bacha; tel: 0524-38 64 00; Tue–Sun dinner only; $$$$

Situated in an accessible spot in the Mouassine district, Dar Moha is one of the city's most celebrated restaurants. This 19th-century riad, with garden and poolside dining options, serves innovative set menus of Moroccan fusion cuisine. Worth the splurge.

Dar el Yacout

79 Sidi Ahled Soussi; tel: 0524-38 29 29; Tue–Sun dinner only; $$$$

Ranked among Marrakesh's finest restaurants, this beautiful medina house, adorned with magnificent stucco and cedar ceilings, serves set menus to satisfy even the most discerning palate. Delicious salad selections, followed by tajines and couscous, are rounded off with superb Moroccan pastries.

Dar Zellij

Kaasour Sidi Benslimane; tel: 0524-38 26 27; Wed–Mon lunch and dinner; $$$$

If you're staying in the northern medina and you don't fancy the long walk through the souks, then Dar Zellij provides a pleasant option for those in search of Moroccan cuisine in a riad setting. Indoor and outdoor dining options; reservations essential.

Le Foundouk

55 Souk Hal Fassi, Kat Bennahid; tel: 0524-37 81 90; daily lunch and dinner; $$$

Hidden in a maze of alleyways and caravanserais in the northern medina, French-owned Le Foundouk is fashionable and atmospheric, serving excellent French and Moroccan cuisine in a wow-factor setting. Open throughout the day (until late), it is always packed to the rafters.

Jemaa el Fna foodstalls

Jemaa el Fna; daily dinner only; $

For an authentic experience, pull up a stool with the locals in the Jemaa el Fna square. At these highly animated outdoor eateries expect anything from sheep's heads to snails in a spicy sauce. Less adventurous diners may decide to stick to delicious brochettes (skewers), chips and salad.

Mama Ti Lee

13 Derb El Arsa, Riad Zitoun Jdid; tel: 0524-38 17 52; dinner only; $$$

Although it is slightly tricky to find, in the medina, once you've located this place you'll be glad you did. It is the perfect spot for a romantic, hidden-away night out. The cuisine is French – the restaurant is owned by French chef Cécile Marot – and the setting is contemporary chic, plus there's a terrace. No alcohol, however. Booking is compulsory.

Price guide for a three-course meal for one, excluding drinks:	
$$$$	over 500DH
$$$	250–500DH
$$	100–250DH
$	under 100DH

Palais Gharnata

5–6 Derb el Arsa, Rue Riad Zitoun el Jdid; tel: 0524-38 96 15; daily lunch and dinner; $$$$

If entertainment in an overblown Moroccan setting with all the orientalist bells and whistles is your thing, then the Palais Gharnata is unlikely to disappoint. In this fiercely traditional palace-style restaurant you can dine on Moroccan cuisine and be entertained by teams of belly dancers and local musicians. Not surprisingly, it is very popular with large tour groups.

Le Pavillon

Derb Zaouia, Bab Doukkala Mosque; tel: 0524-38 70 40; daily dinner only; $$$

For refined French cuisine in the medina, there are few better options than to pay a visit to Le Pavillon. Here you'll be served haute cuisine in a sumptuous, tree-shaded courtyard, a true oasis of calm sheltered from the noise of the medina over the walls. It is located close to Dar el Pacha, and can be accessed by taxi.

Le Riad Monceau

7 Derb Chaabane, Riad Zitoun Lakdim; tel: 0524-42 96 46; www.riad-monceau.com; $$$

This highly recommended converted riad has a cookery school and particularly fine restaurant, which serves sophisticated and delicate Moroccan dishes in a romantic atmosphere in a courtyard overlooking the riad swimming pool. Alcohol is served. Booking ahead usually essential.

La Sultana

Rue de la Kasbah; tel: 0524-38 80 08; daily dinner only; $$$$

Non-guests are welcomed for dinner at this glorious boutique hotel. There are views over the Saadian Tombs from the roof terrace, and you can dine on specialities such as duck foie gras with apples from Ourika or leg of lamb with honey tajine. Book ahead.

Tatchibana

38 Route de Bab Ksiba; tel: 0524-38 71 71; Wed–Sun lunch and dinner, Tue dinner only; $$–$$$

Situated in the Kasbah district is this surprising find. That it now has a Japanese restaurant is testament to how cosmopolitan Marrakesh has become nowadays. A peaceful haven serving excellent set menus and à la carte Japanese dishes.

Terrasse des Epices

15 Souq Cherifia; tel: 0524-37 59 04; lunch and dinner; $$

Charming medina terrace with a view, offering Moroccan salads, tagines, fries, and other such tasty snacks.

Le Tobsil

22 Derb Moulay Abdellah Ben Hassaien, Bab Ksour R'mila; tel: 0524-44 40 52; Wed–Mon dinner only; closed Aug; $$$$

The well-known Tobsil offers excellent Moroccan food in a beautiful riad that has been lovingly restored by its French owner. The set menu here consists of a number of courses of finely prepared Moroccan staples,

Above from far left: chefs at work on a foodstall in the Jemaa el Fna; dining in an atmospheric riad courtyard.

Opening Times
Moroccans tend to eat later than northern Europeans. Restaurant opening times resemble those of southern Europe, with lunch taken between 1pm and 3pm and dinner served from 8pm until around 11pm. The swisher restaurants in the medina tend to open for dinner only, so for lunch you're advised to head to the New Town, where restaurants cater to a mixed crowd of tourists and local office workers.

The growth of tourism, and general affluence, in Marrakesh has made the city an increasingly popular place to eat out, so you are advised to make reservations at most of the restaurants listed. You can usually find a table available at lunchtimes, but in the evenings the city's more popular restaurants can be very crowded.

all served with grace against a background of traditional *gnaoua* music.

Villa Flore

4 Derb Azzouz; tel: 0524-39 17 00; lunch and dinner; $$$

In an elegant converted riad, delicate cuisine is served at sun-shaded tables in a graceful, hidden-away courtyard home. This is just the place to disappear to savour a long lunch and a glass of wine after spending a busy morning in the souks.

Guéliz/Hivernage

Le 6

Avenue Mohammed VI, Hivernage; tel: 0524-44 91 59; daily lunch and dinner; $$

If you are staying in the Hivernage district, Le 6 is a reliable local option, more of a bar and popular with expats. This bistro serves well-prepared international staples (pizza, pasta, steak and fish), with outdoor and indoor dining possible.

Le 16

Guéliz Plaza, Guéliz; daily lunch only; $

Looking for a light lunch in the heart of the Guéliz shopping district? This popular spot serves good sandwiches and tasty salads and is one of the city's

only cafés with a truly modern European feel.

Afric 'n' Chic

6 Rue Oum Errabia, Guéliz; tel: 0524-43 14 24; Mon–Sat dinner only; $$

For live music with your meal, Afric 'n' Chic, a busy place run by one of the city's few Brazilian residents, is a good choice for dinner. The menu is international and the music, served up by the house band, is, unsurprisingly, Latin. Open late.

Al-Fassia

55 Boulevard Zerktouni, Guéliz; tel: 0524-43 40 60; daily dinner only; $$–$$$

One of Marrakesh's most popular medium-priced Moroccan restaurants, Al-Fassia, with its all-female cooking and waiting staff, serves perhaps the best Moroccan home-cooking in town. All the favourites take their place on an extensive menu, which includes such delights as chicken with caramelised pumpkin and sweet pigeon pie.

Brochette Grills

Rue ibn Aicha, Guéliz; daily lunch and dinner; $

In the street between the Montecristo Café and the Rue Casablanca (heralded by the smoke and smell of barbecued meat), a row of simple restaurants with pavement seating serve cuts of meat barbecued in open kitchens. Just select the meat you want at the counter and take a seat. Cheap, fresh and very tasty.

Price guide for a three-course meal for one, excluding drinks:	
$$$$	over 500DH
$$$	250–500DH
$$	100–250DH
$	under 100DH

Casanova

221 Avenue Yacoub el Mansour, Guéliz; tel: 0524-42 37 35; daily lunch and dinner; $$

As one of the newest, and best, Italian restaurants in Marrakesh, Casanova serves high-quality Italian food with its roots in Venetian cuisine. Owned, run and patronised by Italians (a good sign), with indoor and outdoor dining facilities, this simply furnished restaurant offers good value for money and food made with excellent imported ingredients and wines.

Catanzaro

42 Rue Tarik ibn Ziad, Guéliz; tel: 0524-43 37 31; Mon–Sat lunch and dinner; $$

Catanzaro, along with Bagatelle, is arguably the best-known restaurant in the New Town. Serving a wide range of moderately priced pizzas and pasta dishes, this expat hangout is very popular. The food is unremarkable but the atmosphere makes the place a one-off. Book ahead.

Le Chat qui Rit

92 Rue de Yougoslavie, Guéliz; tel: 0524-43 43 11; Tue–Sun dinner; $$

Popular and reasonably priced Franco-Italian backstreet restaurant, with a menu that boasts enough variety to satisfy most tastes. Recommended for a cheap and unpretentious night out.

Le Comptoir

Avenue Echaouada, Hivernage; tel: 0524-43 77 02; daily dinner only; $$$–$$$$

Probably Marrakesh's most famous nightspot, Le Comptoir is as exotic a venue as the city has to offer. It is not noted particularly for its cuisine, but this bar/restaurant serves Moroccan meals to a backbeat of ambient Arabic music, all accompanied by the obligatory belly-dancing floorshow amid what, it must be admitted, is a beautiful decor. For a group night out Le Comptoir is hard to beat. It's always busy, so it's best to book ahead.

Le Grand Café de la Poste

Corner of Boulevard Mansour Eddahbi and Avenue l'Imam Malik, Guéliz; tel: 0524-43 30 38; daily from 8am; $$$

Situated next to the main post office on Place de 16 Novembre, this brasserie-cum-café occupies an old 1920s building. It offers breakfast from 8am, light lunches, ice cream, cakes and pastries in the afternoon, and modern European choices for dinner. Live music most evenings.

Le Jacaranda

32 Boulevard Zerktouni, Guéliz; tel: 0524-24 72 15; daily lunch and dinner; $$$

Classic French cuisine in the heart of Guéliz. This popular, simple restaurant, which dates back to the 1950s and the era of the Protectorate, is a good bet for well-prepared and tasty food.

Le Jardin des Arts

6 Rue Sakia El Hamra, Semlalia; tel: 0524-44 66 34; Mon dinner only, Tue–Sat lunch and dinner; $$$

Above from far left: smart waiting staff; as well as classic Moroccan cuisine you can find modern European cooking; choosing the wine at Le Comptoir; sweets filled with almond paste.

Le Jardin des Arts, situated just off the Casablanca road in Semlalia (north of Guéliz), offers innovative, sophisticated French cuisine served in a modernist Moroccan setting and in an attractive garden. There are good-value menus and à la carte dining.

Palais Jad Mahal

Fontaine de la Mamounia, Hivernage; tel: 0524-43 69 84; daily dinner only; $$$

This is a lavish oriental palace restaurant in the Hivernage offering excellent international/Moroccan fusion cuisine and a floorshow of belly dancers and music. Even with the belly-dancing routine it is all very tasteful, very chic, and, although the food is not especially expensive, a few drinks in the bar will make a hefty dent in your wallet.

Puerto Banus

Rue ibn Hanbal, Hivernage; tel: 0524-44 65 34; daily lunch and dinner; $$$

A long-established fish restaurant in a Spanish-style villa, which is set in a garden with a patio for outside dining in summer. Wonderful oysters from Oualidia, tasty seafood tapas, and a great seafood *pastilla*. Good-value set lunches.

Price guide for a three-course meal for one, excluding drinks:	
$$$$	over 500DH
$$$	250–500DH
$$	100–250DH
$	under 100DH

La Table de Mona

Résidence Isis, 6 Rue du Capitaine Arrighi; tel: 06-18 13 79 59; Mon–Sat lunch and dinner; $$

This friendly, rose-pink restaurant offers tasty Lebanese cooking that's ideal for snacking and sharing. They have a choice of selected mezze, including a highly recommended *babaganoush*. There's an attractive small garden, too.

La Trattoria de Giancarlo

179 Rue Mohamed Beqal, Gueliz; tel: 0524-43 26 41; dinner daily; $$$–$$$$

In a charming villa that mixes 1920s and Moroccan style, this lovely oasis, with its opulent garden, serves scrumptious Italian cuisine from a menu that travels from Bologna to Tuscany and beyond. Lots of pasta, meat and fish dishes.

The Palmeraie

Dar Ennasim

Le Pavillon du Golf, Palmeraie Golf Palace, Circuit de la Palmeraie; tel: 0524-33 43 08; daily lunch and dinner; $$$$

Run by Fabrice Vulin, the proud possessor of two Michelin stars, this is a restaurant for foodies and those celebrating a really special occasion. The restaurant is situated beside a pool on the Palmeraie golf course, and has a lovely verandah for dining alfresco. The interior is sleek and modern, with statement furniture and contemporary art on the walls. The delicious modern European food is

inventive, often with a Moroccan twist. Fish features prominently on the menu.

L'Abyssin

Hotel Palais Rhoul, Route de Fez; tel: 0524-32 94 94; daily dinner only; $$$$

L'Abyssin, with its all-white decor and candlelit walkways, is one of the city's most fashionable restaurants. Situated in the grounds of the Palais Rhoul Hotel, in the Palmeraie district, this ultra-hip, oriental-style restaurant serves a mix of Asian dishes and a range of sophisticated international dishes. Pricey but special.

Amanjena

Amanjena Hotel, Route d'Ouarzazate; tel: 0524-40 33 53; daily lunch and dinner; $$$$

For Thai cuisine and a good look at the interior of the most extravagant hotel in Marrakesh, head for the restaurant at this hotel in the Amelkis golf complex. The restaurant is situated alongside the swimming pool. Booking essential.

Bo-Zin

Route de l'Ourika, km 3.5; tel: 0524-38 80 12; daily dinner only; $$$

Despite its situation in a nondescript village on the Ourika road (on the edge of town), dimly lit Bo-Zin is the height of Marrakesh chic. *The* restaurant for local movers and shakers, this haven of cool serves a range of specialities from Moroccan to Thai cuisine.

Le Crystal

Pacha Marrakech, Boulevard Mohammed VI; tel: 0524-38 84 80; www.pachamarrakech.com; daily dinner only; $$$$

The highly acclaimed Crystal is one of the two places to eat at the mind-boggling Pacha club. It serves its own version of a refined Mediterranean cuisine. Among the delicious options on the menu, tuna carpaccio and *moelleux au chocolat* are some of the chef's specialities.

La Ferme Berbère

Douar Touggana, Route de l'Ourika, km 9; tel: 0524-38 56 85; daily lunch and dinner; $$

Although it is not especially noted for its fine cuisine, this agreeable spot serves basic Moroccan fare in a grassy garden with a pool and views out to the High Atlas Mountains. As it is not exactly central, it's a good bet for a long, lazy lunch and a post-lunch lounge. You must reserve in advance.

Le Touggana

Route de l'Ourika, km 9; tel: 0524-37 62 78; Mon and Wed–Fri dinner only, Sat–Sun lunch and dinner; $$$

Formerly the restaurant 'KM9', Touggana makes for an excellent evening out if you fancy escaping Marrakesh for a while. The French-based cuisine is served in an attractive dining room with patio doors that give out on to a bougainvillea-filled terrace. There's also a well-stocked bar for an *apéritif* or *digestif*. Only *grands taxis* will take you this far out of town.

Above from far left: alcohol laws have been relaxed and late-night drinking spots have sprung up in the medina; fresh fish restaurants in Essaouira.

Admission to clubs ranges from 150–400DH, and includes a drink. Traditional bars are still male preserves, but there is an increasing choice of other places: often bars double up as restaurants, and some cafés now serve alcoholic drinks. For live music, any night on the Jemaa el Fna there is *gnaoua* music and dance, and many restaurants feature live music with dinner. Check the free monthly *Couleurs Marrakech* (www.couleurs-marrakech.com).

Music Venues

Dar Cherifa
8 Derb Chorfa el-Kebir; tel: 0524-42 64 63

Occasional concerts and cultural evenings in this restored riad-café.

Institut Français
Route de la Targa, outskirts of Guéliz; tel: 0524-44 69 30; www.ifm.ma

Occasional concerts of Moroccan or French music.

Kechmara
1bis–3 Rue de la Liberté, Guéliz; tel: 0524-42 25 32; www.kechmara.ma; Mon–Sat noon–midnight;

Popular restaurant and bar, packed on Wednesdays and Fridays at 7.30pm when there is good live music.

Kosybar
47 Place des Ferblantiers, Southern Medina; tel: 0524-38 03 24; daily noon–midnight;

This trendy piano bar has live jazz on weekend evenings.

Taros
Place Moulay Hassan, Essaouira; tel: 0524-47 64 07; www.taroscafe.com; Mon–Sat 11am–4pm, 6pm–midnight

Live music every night on the rooftop terrace at this funky yet chilled place.

Théâtre Royal
40 Boulevard Mohammed VI, Guéliz; tel: 0524-43 15 16

Has a splendid outdoor amphitheatre where regular performances of theatre and dance are held.

Bars

Bo&Zin
Douar Lahna, Route de l'Ourika, 3.5km (2 miles); tel: 0524-38 80 12; http://bo-zin.com; daily 8pm–1am or later

This stylish DJ bar really gets going after midnight, particularly at weekends. Popular outdoor bar in summer.

Café Arabe
184 Rue Mouassine, Mouassine Quarter; tel: 0524-42 97 28; www.cafearabe.com; daily 10am–midnight

Another atmospheric rooftop and *zellij*-clad courtyard where you can relax with a drink. Avoid the food though, it's mediocre.

Le Comptoir
Rue Echouhada, Hivernage; tel: 0524-43 77 02; www.comptoirdarna.com; daily 8pm–1am

The most happening bar in town, good for a cocktail after dinner.

Grand Café de la Poste

Corner of Boulevard Mansour Eddahbi and Avenue Imam Malik, Guéliz; tel: 0524-43 30 38; www. grandcafedelaposte.com; daily 8am–11pm

The upstairs bar lounge has a DJ every evening; it is *the* meeting place in town, and is good for a relaxed drink.

Terrasse des Epices

15 Souk Cherifia, Dar el Bacha, Mouassine Quarter; tel: 0524-37 59 04; www.terrassedesepices.com; daily 10am–midnight

Terrasse des Epices is the coolest rooftop to hang out on in the medina, with great music and food.

Casino de Marrakesh

Hotel Es Saadi and Casino, Avenue el Kadissia, Hivernage; tel: 0524-44 88 11; www.essaadi.com; Sun–Thur 7pm–4am, Fri–Sat 7pm–5am

Grand casino, as well established as the hotel, for the rich and famous.

Grand Casino de la Mamounia

Avenue Bab Jedid, Hivernage; tel: 0524-44 45 70; www.grandcasino mamounia.com; daily 9pm–5am;

Splendid Art Deco casino next door to the famous La Mamounia hotel.

Day Clubs

Nikki Beach

Circuit de la Palmeraie, Guéliz; tel: 0663-51 99 92; www.nikkibeach. com; mid-Mar–Jan

With a hip Ibiza-meets-St-Tropez atmosphere, this is the hottest day club in town. Dress to impress.

Plage Rouge

Km 10, route de l'Ourika; tel: 0524-37 80 86; www.ilove-marrakesh. com/laplagerouge; daily noon–1am

DJs spin their non-stop house music by the large pool, but children and families are welcome.

Nightclubs

Cantobar

38 Boulevard Moulay Hassan, Guéliz; tel: 0524-43 33 50; www.cantobar-marrakech.com; daily 7.30pm–4am; free if you have dinner and drinks

Bar-restaurant-nightclub with popular karaoke nights on the stage for a relaxing night out.

Diamant Noir

Hotel Marrakesh, corner Avenue Mohammed V and Rue Oum Errabia, Guéliz; tel: 0524-43 43 51; daily 10pm–4am; admission charge

Old-fashioned, kitsch nightclub with hip-hop and *Marrakeshi* tunes. Gay-friendly on weekend nights.

Pacha Marrakesh

Boulevard Mohammed VI, Hivernage; tel: 0524-38 84 05; www. pachamarrakesh.com; daily 8pm–5am; admission charge after 10pm

Enormous complex with several restaurants, lounges and a large clubbing area with international and local DJs. Best at weekends as it's less busy during the week.

Above from far left: fiddle players and clubbers – something to suit all tastes.

CREDITS

Insight Step by Step Marrakesh
Written by: Dorothy Stannard and
Charlie Shepherd.
Updated by: Abigail Hole
Edited by: Alex Knights
Series Editor: Clare Peel
Cartography Editors: Zoë Goodwin and
James Macdonald
Picture Manager: Steven Lawrence
Art Editors: Ian Spick, Richard Cooke
Production: Linton Donaldson
Photography by: Apa: Clay Perry, Tony Halliday,
Phil Wood except: Alamy 23B, 23TR, 42-43, 47B,
58T, 65T, 69B; Ciel d'Afrique 22B; Corbis 13B,
81TR; Getty 20T, 50ML, 57TL, 65B, 97B;
iStockphoto 11TL, 13TR, 24B, 25TL, 32TR,
36ML, 42BL, 46TL, 48T, 52M, 52B; Kobal 87B;
Les Jardins de la Medina 25b; Mary Evans 26T,
27T; Corrie Wingate 71TR, 100TR.
Cover: main image: Four Corners; bottom left and
right: iStockphoto; back cover: Fotolia.

Printed by: CTPS-China

CONTACTING THE EDITORS

We would appreciate it if readers would alert us
to errors or outdated information by writing to
us at insight@apaguide.co.uk or Apa Publications,
PO Box 7910, London SE1 1WE, UK.

www.insightguides.com

DISTRIBUTION

Worldwide

**APA Publications GmbH & Co. Verlag KG
(Singapore branch)**
7030 Ang Mo Kio Ave 5
08-65 Northstar @ AMK
Singapore 569880
Email: apasin@singnet.com.sg

UK and Ireland

GeoCenter International Ltd
Meridian House
Churchill Way West
Basingstoke
Hampshire RG21 6YR
Email: sales@geocenter.co.uk

US

Ingram Publisher Services
One Ingram Blvd
PO Box 3006
La Vergne, TN 37086-1986
Email: customer.service@ingrampublisherservices.com

Australia

Universal Publishers
1 Waterloo Road
Macquarie Park
NSW 2113
Email: sales@universalpublishers.com.au

New Zealand

Hema Maps New Zealand Ltd (HNZ)
Unit 2
10 Cryers Road
East Tamaki
Auckland 2013
Email: sales.hema@clear.net.nz

INDEX

Around Marrakech